A Guide to Jewish Genealogy in Lithuania

No. 6 in the Jewish Ancestor Series

GW00541179

by

Sam Aaron

Co-ordinator of the LitvakSIG's Raseiniai District Research Group
Member of the JGSGB Lithuania SIG

זכר ימות עולם בינו שנות דר-ודר
שאל אביך ויגדך זקניך ויאמרו-לך :

Remember the days of old, consider the years of many generations:
Ask thy father, and he will declare unto thee: Thine elders, and they will tell thee.

Deuteronomy XXXII v.7   דברים לב ז

Published by
The Jewish Genealogical Society of Great Britain
Registered Charity No. 1022738
PO Box 13288, London, N3 3WD. England, U.K.
E-mail: publications@jgsgb.org.uk
Web site: www.jgsgb.org.uk

First edition August 2005

Copyright © Sam Aaron

ISBN: 0 9537669 8 5

Front cover designed by
Rosemary Hoffman and Derek Wenzerul

Printed and bound in the United Kingdom
by the Alden Group Ltd., Oxford
☎ 01865 253200

CONTENTS

THE JEWISH GENEALOGICAL SOCIETY OF GREAT BRITAIN (JGSGB)

The JGSGB is the premier society for Jewish genealogy in Great Britain. The Society encourages genealogical research and promotes the preservation of Jewish genealogical records and resources. It provides a forum for sharing information amongst members.

Membership is open to both beginners and to more experienced researchers. Members have the opportunity to meet likeminded people at central meetings, regional meetings, group meetings and at informal meetings in members' homes.

GENERAL ENQUIRIES
JGSGB, PO Box 13288, London, N3 3WD. England. U.K.
E-mail: **enquiries@jgsgb.org.uk**
Web-site: **www.jgsgb.org.uk**

MEMBERSHIP ENQUIRIES
The Membership Secretary, PO Box 2508,
Maidenhead, SL6 8WS. England, U.K.
E-mail: **membership@jgsgb.org.uk**

PUBLICATIONS
JGSGB Publications, PO Box 180, St. Albans,
Herts. AL2 3WH. England. U.K.
E-mail: **publications@jgsgb.org.uk**

MEMBERS' GENEALOGICAL RESOURCE LIBRARY
Finchley Synagogue, Kinloss Gardens, Finchley, London, N3 2SY.
The library contains extensive information and genealogical resources including several hundred reference books, computers and a selection of genealogical CD-ROMs and other genealogical databases. IT helpers are on hand to assist. It also houses a large collection of maps and leaflets as well as microfilms and microfiches (including copies of many of the major Anglo-Jewish genealogy collections). The members' library has one of the largest collections of Yizkor (Memorial) books in the UK. (For opening times contact the Society.)

FOR BEGINNERS
Family history workshops, One-to-one mentoring scheme, Research guidance, Publications and Computer courses.

EXPERIENCED RESEARCHERS
Extensive library, Annual seminar, Special interest groups, Research visits and Genealogical workshops.

FOR EVERYONE
Regular newsletter, Quarterly journal *Shemot*, Online discussion group, Monthly meetings, Regional groups, Members only website, JGSGB family finder, Informal meetings at home.

WEB-SITE www.jgsgb.org.uk
Our website has a resource-packed section reserved for JGSGB members only and links to almost every conceivable genealogical website.

JGSGB JOURNAL
Shemot is the Journal of The Jewish Genealogical Society of Great Britain.

It is published quarterly and is free to members of the Society. Individual copies of any issue of *Shemot* may be purchased from:

> The Jewish Genealogical Society of Great Britain
> PO Box 13288, LONDON, N3 3WD. ENGLAND. U.K.
> E-mail: jgsgb@org.uk   Web site: www.jgsgb.org.uk

If you are trying to trace *Shemot* in a public library, it may help to quote the international reference number ISSN 0969-2258.

Shemot contains articles of a genealogical nature, which range from the personal experiences of an individual member including research methods and sources used to papers on specific areas of research. The JGSGB web site contains a complete list of articles.

AUTHOR'S NOTE

A few preliminary comments on the scope of this guide are necessary.

- Readers of the guide are likely to be amongst the second- or even third-generations of descendants of immigrants from Lithuania. That is to say, their parents or even grandparents may already have been born in the countries in which they are now living. Researching their ancestry will for them therefore involve collecting data about these immigrant parents or grandparents, as well as about the earlier generations that actually lived in Lithuania.

  This guide is concerned primarily with the latter aspect of genealogical research. Its main purpose is to tell the reader what old Lithuanian records are available, where to find them, and how to use them in tracing ancestors who lived in Lithuania. It is beyond the scope of this work to describe in detail where to find similar materials about ancestors who had already settled in countries outside Lithuania, save to the extent that these materials may provide clues or leads to the earlier generations back in the home country.

- The guide is limited in its geographical scope. Jews from Lithuania are commonly referred to as *Litvaks,* and the country from which they originate as *Lite.* But *Lite* did not encompass the same area as the present state of Lithuania, which came into being as an independent state only after the first World War; it was a much larger entity. It was a large area in the west of the Russian empire which included not only present-day Lithuania, but which stretched from the Baltic to the Black Sea, and included also parts of what are now Latvia, Poland, Belarus and Ukraine.

While the more general parts of the guide will apply equally to research into Jewish ancestry in any part of Eastern Europe, as regards specific communities and the archival records which relate to them, it deals only with those towns and *shtetlach* which existed in the area encompassed by the present-day state of Lithuania. The Pale of Settlement was divided into 25 provinces (10 of which were in the so-called "Kingdom of Poland"); only two of the twenty-five (Vilna and Kovno), and part of a third (Suvalki), are in present-day Lithuania. For information on communities now in Latvia, Poland or Belarus and the records pertaining to them, the reader is referred to works on those countries, and to the special interest groups conducting research into those specific areas.

- Most of the records that concern researchers will have been made at a time when the area was still part of the Russian empire, and the names of towns and districts found in those records will therefore be the old Russian names (e.g., Vilna and Kovno), and not the new Lithuanian names for the same towns or districts (Vilnius and Kaunas). The Lithuanian archives use the current Lithuanian names. In this guide I have in the main used the current Lithuanian names, but have retained the old Russian names when I considered that appropriate to the context.

- The resources available to researchers have increased dramatically over the past five years and will no doubt continue to do so. This guide endeavours to provide a comprehensive catalogue of the resources available in the first half of 2005. But it is only a snapshot of the current position: there will always be new resources becoming available, and the URLs of websites listed here will no doubt change from time to time.

ACKNOWLEDGMENTS

I am grateful to Howard Margol, Saul Issroff and Judith Diamond, who read the manuscript in draft and made helpful comments, and to Galina Baranova and David and Sonia Hoffmann, who provided answers to my queries. Any errors that remain are solely my responsibility.

I would also thank Neville Samuels, Nancy Holden, Ellen Kellman and Judith Diamond who made images available.

Finally, my thanks are due to Sylvia McCallum and Rosemary and Derek Wenzerul for their advice on technical matters and their assistance in preparing the text for publication. They were a very patient and supportive team.

1

SOME BASIC HISTORY

Knowledge of the basic facts regarding the history of Lithuania will probably be helpful to someone setting out to research his ancestral roots in that country, and a short summary is therefore given here. As the archival records currently available do not go back beyond about 1760, the emphasis will be on events since that date, but to put these into perspective a brief outline of earlier events is also provided. Readers who wish to know more about the history should consult one of the sources mentioned at the end of this chapter.

Early history: the first Jews in Lithuania

It is thought that Jews first came to Lithuania during the 13th century. The 12th and 13th centuries were the age of the Crusades, and as the bands of crusaders passed through the cities of western Europe on their way to the Holy Land, they massacred Jews found in those cities. In 1264 King Boleslaw V of Poland issued a charter giving Jews his protection, and many moved into Poland to escape the atrocities of the crusaders. It was probably during these times that the first Jews moved also into the area now known as Lithuania.

This was roughly the same time as Lithuania was coming into being as a political entity, as it was during the period 1236-63 that Duke Mindaugas (Mindowe) established Lithuania as a political union between a number of ethnic tribes.

The new state's early history was characterised by continual battles with invading German crusaders (the Teutonic Knights). Grand Duke Gediminas (Gedimin), who ruled the country from 1316 to 1341, started the long-term expansion of Lithuania into the lands of the eastern Slavs. He founded the modern capital city of Vilnius and started the Gediminaiciai dynasty, whose representatives became members of many European monarchies.

Grand Duke Vytautas (Witold the Great) (1392 to 1430) brought military and political prosperity to the country. During his reign, the push eastward by the Teutonic Order was broken. The old Lithuanian state was a tolerant one and more liberal in its attitude to minorities than the other European powers of the time. Vytautas granted Jews privileges in 1388 and 1389 which afforded them equality of religious and civil rights and exempted synagogue and cemetery land from taxes.

In the 14th and 15th centuries Jews were expelled from a number of towns in Germany and Italy, and in 1492 came the expulsion from Spain. The result was a large movement of Jewish communities eastwards, ultimately to Poland, Lithuania and the Ukraine. By the end of the 15th century there were already several towns with Jewish communities in those areas. Despite the odd expulsion even there, (in 1495 the Jews were expelled from Lithuania) the Jews managed to remain in the area, and by 1500 Poland was regarded as the safest country in Europe for Jews. Movement further eastwards was blocked, as under Czar Ivan IV Vasilievich (Ivan the Terrible) Jews were officially excluded from Russian territory.

During the first quarter of the 15th Century, Vytautas extended the borders of Lithuania all the way to the shores of the Black Sea, and by the middle of the century Lithuania was one of the most powerful states in Eastern Europe, stretching from the Baltic to the Black Sea.

The Polish–Lithuanian alliance

In 1569 Lithuania signed the Union of Lublin with Poland. This agreement created a Commonwealth Republic of two nations (the Kingdom of Poland and the Grand Duchy of Lithuania) which shared a joint legislature and one king (who also held the title of Grand Duke of Lithuania). Although the Grand Duchy was in reality a subordinate member in the Polish-Lithuanian confederation, it was strictly speaking a distinct sovereign state, with its own laws, currency and army, and an equal partner with Poland.

Jewish settlers played a substantial role in establishing Poland and the interior of Lithuania, particularly in developing new wheat-growing areas, providing mills and river transport, and developing a foreign trade. A number of new villages grew up in which the Jewish community was an important element.

The first record of Jews in Vilnius dates back to 1567. In 1593 they gained the right to own buildings in the city, although they were allowed to inhabit only a number of specified streets. By 1784 there were around 5,000 Jews in Vilnius. Religious thought developed very intensively: in the second half of 17th century there were forty prominent rabbis living in the city. In the 18th century the great genius, the Gaon of Vilna, Elijah ben Shlomo Zalman, emerged. Vilnius was a recognized spiritual center, and became known as the Jerusalem of Lithuania. It was for some time the main seat of Jewish culture in the whole of Europe.

During the 18th century there was a large movement of Jews into what later became Kaunas *guberniya* from the eastern and southern parts of the Grand Duchy, having been driven out of the large towns of Grodno, Brest-Litovsk and Vilnius by the local non-Jewish populations.

The Partition of the Republic of Lithuania-Poland: incorporation of Lithuania into the Russian empire

From 1654 to 1667 the Grand Duchy of Lithuania had been enmeshed in wars with the growing power of Russia. It had increasing disagreements with Poland, and during the second half of the 18th century it lost nearly all its sovereign rights. Ultimately Russia engaged together with Austria and Prussia in the partition of the Polish-Lithuanian Republic. There were three such partitions: in 1772, 1793 and 1795. Following the third partition, Poland ceased to exist as a state, and the major part of the former Grand Duchy of Lithuania was handed over to Russia. The number of Jews in the Polish-Lithuanian Republic immediately before the partitions is estimated to have been about 250,000, with 10,000-15,000 living in the area that is today Lithuania.

At first things went smoothly for the Lithuanians. Vilnius (named Vilna by the Russians) was the third largest city in the Russian Empire (after Moscow and St Petersburg) and retained its grandeur.

3

But a change of direction came in 1812, with Napoleon's campaign against Russia. The French were enthusiastically received in Lithuania as liberators, but the retreat that followed soon after was the prelude to disaster. Czar Nicholas I initiated a new policy: the authorities began to Russify the area and to transform it into a provincial hinterland.

The position of the Jewish population underwent a major change. With the annexation of large portions of Poland as a result of the three partitions at the end of the 18th century, a large number of Jews were introduced into the Russian population. They were unwanted. Until then there had not been many Jews in Russia, and the need to adjust to this sudden influx presented a problem to the Czars, who did not want the new arrivals to mingle with the rest of the population. This resulted in a number of decrees restricting their rights.

First there were three decrees by Catherine the Great in 1783, 1791 and 1794 which restricted the commercial rights of Jews to the areas newly annexed. In 1804 Alexander I issued the first of a series of statutes regulating where the Jews could live (the Pale of Settlement), and what they could do there. By 1812, the Pale of Settlement had taken its final form, comprising 15 provinces (*gubernii*) stretching from the Baltic to the Black Sea, and including the areas now known as Latvia, Lithuania, Belarus and the Ukraine, plus another 10 *gubernii* in the erstwhile Kingdom of Poland. The Jewish population, with few exceptions, was now restricted to living in the Pale. Moreover, they could not own land, and could no longer live in the villages. They had to move into the small towns that we now know as the *shtetlach*. Although they were living in what was primarily an agricultural economy, they could no longer engage in agriculture. They had to become tailors, cobblers, pedlars and small shopkeepers. Only merchants of the top guild, people with higher or special education, artisans, soldiers and their descendants were permitted to live outside the Pale.

The Lithuanians revolted twice against the occupiers, in 1831 and 1863, but were unsuccessful. The consequences were that Vilna University and other institutions of higher education were closed, the influence of the Catholic Church was curbed, and the Russian

Orthodox Religion was declared the state religion. Lithuanians were not permitted to purchase land, or erect new churches. The centuries-old ties between Lithuania and Central and Western Europe were broken. The cultural life of the country went into a state of paralysis. From 1864 the Lithuanian language itself and its Latin alphabet were banned and the so-called *grazdanka*, Lithuanian with the Russian alphabet, was introduced.

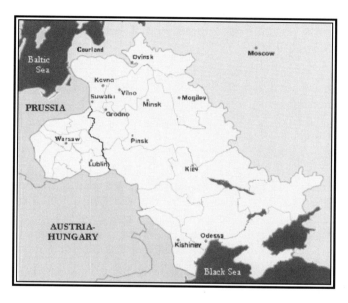

The Pale of Settlement

Towards the end of the 19th century a struggle for national culture and for the re-institution of writing spread over the greater part of the country. Lithuanian books in the Latin alphabet were printed in Prussia, under German jurisdiction, and illegally transported across the border into Lithuania. It was not until 1904 that Lithuanian representatives managed to win the lifting of the ban on Lithuanian publications and educational institutions.

There was again a large movement of Jews into Lithuania proper during the 19th century from eastern and southern parts of what had been the Grand Duchy. This is something to be borne in mind as you trace your roots back in time; your ancestors may not always have lived in the same *shtetl* or even the same area. However, a series of pogroms in Russia in the 1870s and 1880s (although there were never any in Lithuania until 1905) led to mass emigration to the United States.

By 1897 there were nearly 300,000 Jews living in the Pale, but because of the restrictions on them, most of them were living in great poverty. There were about 63,000 Jews in Vilna, representing approximately 45 percent of the population. The Pale lasted until World War I, and was formally abolished by the Provisional Government in 1917.

An illuminating contemporary report (1872) on the legal position of the Hebrews in Czarist Russia by the American Charge d'Affaires in St Petersburg at the time, Eugene Schuyler, can be found on-line at www.angelfire.com/ms2/belaroots/schuyler.htm.

World War I: Lithuania gains its independence

At the start of World War I Russian troops invaded East Prussia, but the German armies soon turned the tide, and Lithuania was occupied by Germany and the Russian armies driven back. In 1915 the Russians, fearing that the Jews might spy for the Germans, who treated then better than the Russians had done, forcibly moved a large portion of the Jewish population (about 100,000) from the Pale to other parts of Russia. Many Jews from north-eastern Lithuania ended up in the Crimea, others in central Russia.

With the end of the war in sight, Eastern and Central Europe were full of ethnic and nationalist movements clamouring for independence. The Czarist regime had been overthrown by the Russian revolution, and a number of new republics were being set up. The Lithuanians made their claim in February 1918 when, even though the German Army and authorities were still in control of the entire country, the elected Council of Lithuania proclaimed the independent state of Lithuania. Many Jews who had been forced to leave, returned.

The Paris Peace Conference in 1919 supported the various claims for the right of self-determination, and the Allies for reasons of their own wanted to re-create a large independent Polish state. In the vicinity of Lithuania, the Belorussians broke away from Russia to establish an independent republic, while in the north Latvia also sought its independence. The consequence was that the map of the entire region was re-drawn, and various parts of what had formerly been western Russian territory were incorporated into the new states. The German port of Memel was given first to the League of Nations, and ultimately passed to Lithuania. The area around Vilna was disputed between Poland and the newly independent Lithuania. Although the Paris Peace Conference assigned the city to the Lithuanians, the Poles refused to give it up, and invaded Russia and Lithuania, occupying Vilna. After a referendum in 1922, it was incorporated into Poland. It remained so until 1940, when Soviet troops occupied the city and transferred it to Lithuania, which was then incorporated into the USSR. From 1920-1940 the capital of Lithuania was Kovno (now re-named Kaunas).

Area of SE Lithuania occupied by Poland from 1918-1939

The new Lithuanian state remained independent throughout the period between the two World Wars. Jewish life in this period was untroubled. On the whole, Jewish communities got on well with their non-Jewish neighbours. In many of the towns, Jews constituted 50 per cent or more of the population. Community life was rich and

7

well organized. There were six daily Jewish newspapers. Vilnius had 105 synagogues and prayer houses.

World War II: Lithuania annexed to the USSR

Just days before World War II broke out in September 1939 the Soviet Union entered into non-aggression and territorial agreements with Nazi Germany, and one of the matters agreed upon was that Lithuania be returned to the Soviet sphere. At that time, Lithuania's Jewish population had grown to about 250,000. This number included about 15,000 Jewish refugees who fled to Vilnius from Nazi-occupied Poland. Most of Lithuania's non-Jewish population was angered by the Nazi-Soviet pact, which took away their country's independence. They let out their anger on the country's Jews with attacks on them and their property.

On June 15, 1940 the Soviet army moved in and took control of Lithuania; about seven weeks later Lithuania was officially annexed to the USSR. Lithuania's Jews were affected profoundly when it became a Soviet republic. The effects were mixed. On one hand, Jewish representatives were asked to join the government, and Jews were allowed to attend institutions of higher learning without restriction. On the other hand, many of their businesses were nationalized, and Jewish political, cultural, and welfare organizations were closed down. On June 14, 1941 the Soviets expelled tens of thousands of Lithuanians whom they considered to be "enemies of the people." Among them were some 7,000 Jews. Although the Jews suffered very greatly under the Soviets, their fellow Lithuanians considered them to be supporters of the Soviets. As a result, many Lithuanians, including members of the nationalist Lithuanian Activist Front, harassed the country's Jews.

The Holocaust in Lithuania

On June 22, 1941 Germany invaded the Soviet Union, including Soviet-held territories such as Lithuania. Most of the Lithuanian population welcomed the Germans, and many willingly collaborated with the German invaders. Even before the Germans finished conquering Lithuania, the Lithuanians carried out pogroms against the Jews in at least 40 localities. Jews were killed, injured and raped, and rabbis were brutalized.

Just weeks after the Germans arrived, they instituted a systematic campaign to exterminate all of Lithuanian Jewry, led by *Einsatzkommando* 3 of *Einsatgruppe* A. During the summer of 1941 most of the Jews of the provinces were murdered, and from September to November most of those in the big cities (who had been imprisoned in ghettos when the Germans arrived) were also slaughtered.

By late 1941 only 40,000 Jews were left in Lithuania; these were localized in four ghettos (in Vilnius, Kaunas, Siauliai, and Svencionys) and several labor camps. During the summer and autumn of 1943 the ghettos in Vilnius and Svencionys were liquidated, while those in Kaunas and Siauliai became concentration camps. Approximately 15,000 Jews were sent to labor camps in Latvia and Estonia, where they perished, and some 5,000 Jews were sent to extermination camps. Before the Germans retreated from Lithuania in the summer of 1944, they transferred about 10,000 Jews from the Kaunas and Siauliai camps to concentration camps in Germany. Those who tried to resist were murdered. By the time Germany surrendered to the Allies in 1945, only a few thousand Lithuanian Jews had survived.

Lithuania reclaims its independence

In March 1990, with the dissolution of the USSR, Lithuania became an independent state once more.

Further reading:

For a useful historical perspective on Lithuanian history see
Chapter I in *Lithuanian Jewish Communities*
Ed: Nancy and Stuart Schoenberg New York, 1991

For a detailed account, see Masha Greenbaum:
The Jews of Lithuania: A History of a Remarkable Community 1316-1945 (1995)

2

ADMINISTRATIVE DIVISIONS

The records now collected in the Lithuanian archives were mostly kept on a town-by-town basis. That is to say, each such record was a list of persons living (or registered) in one particular town (although often persons living in the vicinity of a town, whether in crossroads taverns or settlements too small to merit a list of their own, were included as part of the town's community). But there were also some records kept on a district basis, listing persons living in all the towns in a particular district. So, for example, there was a 1912 list of men who avoided conscription drawn up for the whole district of Raseiniai. This means that when searching the records for a mention of your ancestors, you need to know what *shtetl* they lived in, and also what district the *shetl* was in.

There is an important point to note here. Modern Lithuania is divided into ten administrative divisions, or counties (*apskritys*). But for purposes of genealogical research, your concern is with the administrative divisions that existed in the time of the Russian empire. At that time the country was divided into a large number of provinces (*gubernii* – singular: *guberniya*) which were in turn divided into districts (*uezds*).

You may in the course of your research find that two lists allocate the same town to different "districts". For example, Schoenburg and Schoenburg, in their book on *Lithuanian Jewish Communities* place Rietavas in Telz district. The Yad Vashem Central Database of Shoah Victims does the same. But the Lithuanian Archives place it in Raseiniai district. This is because the first two lists are referring to the districts (*apskritys*) of present-day Lithuania, while the archives place towns in their old Russian *uezds*. What confuses matters further is that some of the current *apskritys* have the same names as some of the old *uezds*, but do not cover the same areas as their name-sake *uezds* did, and therefore even in a case where the old name survived, a town may be listed in two different "districts". For purposes of genealogical research one needs to know the Russian *uezd* in which the *shtetl* was located, as this is the basis upon which the old records were drawn up. To find the Russian *uezd* in which your ancestral *shtetl* was located, consult the list of towns in Appendix A.

The Russian *gubernii* and *uezds*

Modern Lithuania incorporates parts of only three of the old Russian *gubernii,* namely, Kovno, Vilna and Suvalki. Before the outbreak of World War I, the three had been divided into 21 districts, the Russian names of which were as set out below:

Kovno	**Vilna**	**Suvalki**
Kovno	Oshmiany	Augustov
Ponevezh	Disna	Suvalki
Rosseiny	Lida	Kalvaria
Shavli	Sventsiany	Marijampole
Telshi	Troki	Seiny
Vilkomir	Vileika	Vladislavov
Novo-Aleksandrov	Vilna	Volkovishki

But these *uezds* are no longer all within the boundaries of the present state of Lithuania. After World War I, when the map of Central and Eastern Europe was redrawn by the Paris Peace Conference and the Treaty of Versailles, a number of new states were carved out of what had been the Czarist Russian empire. The boundaries fixed for the new states often cut across existing boundaries, with the result that the territory of some *gubernii* was divided between two or more states.

- The southern *guberniya* of Grodno became part of the breakaway Belorussian Democratic Republic. (It was transferred to Poland in 1920, but re-incorporated in 1939 into what had by then become the Belorussian Soviet Socialist Republic. In 1990 this became the independent Republic of Belarus);

- The northern *guberniya* of Courland was incorporated into the new independent state of Latvia;
- Parts of Vilna *guberniya* became part of the new Belorussian republic. These were Disna, Oshmiany and Vileika *uezds*, and part of Lida *uezd*, with only a small part of Lida *uezd* remaining in Vilna *guberniya*;

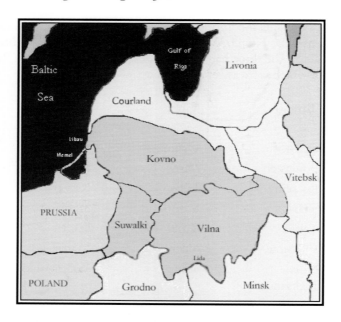

The northern Russian gubernii as they were immediately after World War I

- Part of Novo-Aleksandrov *uezd* (in Kovno *guberniya*) also went to the Belorussian republic, and another small part of it to Latvia;
- Part of Suvalki *guberniya* (the *uezds* of Suvalki and Augustow, later known as Griskabudis, and part of Sejni *uezd*) became part of the new state of Poland;
- The new independent state of Lithuania was created out of the remaining parts of Kovno, Vilna and Suvalki *gubernii*, which were now given the Lithuanian names of Kaunas, Vilnius and Suwalki.

12

It is only with these latter three *gubernii* and their 16 *uezds* that went into the newly constituted state of Lithuania that this guide is concerned. Their new Lithuanian names are given below, followed by the old Russian names in brackets.

Kaunas *guberniya*	Vilnius *guberniya*	Suwalki *guberniya*
Kaunas (Kovno)	Lida (Lida)	Kalvarija (Kalvaria)
Panevezys (Ponevezh)	Svencionys (Sventsiany)	Marijampole (Marijampole)
Raseiniai (Rosseiny)	Trakai (Troki)	Sejny (Seiny)
Sauliai (Shavli)	Vilnius (Vilna)	Kudirkos Naumiestis (Vladislavov)
Telsiai (Telshi)		Vilkaviskis (Volkovishki)
Ukmerge (Vilkomir)		
Zarasai (Novo-Aleksandrov)		

Internal boundary changes and name changes

The gubernii

Even before the boundary changes brought about by the creation of new nation states in 1919, the internal boundaries of the *gubernii* had not always been constant.

The territory of the Grand Duchy of Lithuania that had been incorporated into Czarist Russia in 1795 initially all formed one province, called the Lithuania *guberniya* and later re-named the Vilna *guberniya.* This included all the territory of modern Lithuania, as well as some adjacent territories that were later taken away to be incorporated into the new states of Latvia, Belarus and Poland.

A major reorganization occurred in December 1842, when the Vilna *guberniya* was split into two: a new *guberniya,* named Kovno *guberniya,* with the city of Kovno (Kaunas) as its capital, was formed out of the northern *uezds* of Vilna *guberniya,* namely: Telshi, Shavli, Rosseiny, Upita, Novo-aleksandrovsk, Vilkomir, and part of Kovno. Upita *uezd* was re-named Ponevezh *uezd* after the major city in the district. Part of the Rosseiny *uezd* lying between the river Dubissa and the edge of the Shavli *uezd* were added to Kovno *uezd,* as well as a small piece of land near the town of Rumshishki. (See the article on the creation of the new *guberniya* at <u>www.jewishgen.org/Litvak/createkovno.htm</u>).

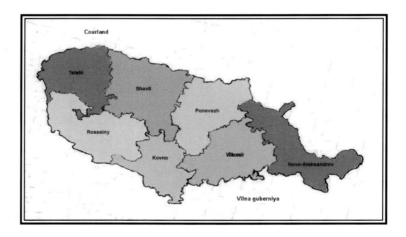

The seven *uezds* of Kovno *guberniya,* created in 1842

To compensate Vilna *guberniya* for the loss of its northern *uezds* to the new Kovno *guberniya,* the Lida *uezd* was taken from Grodno *guberniya,* and the Disna and Vileika *uezds* from Minsk *guberniya,* and these were added to Vilna *guberniya.* The Zavileyski *uezd* was renamed Sventsiany. The city of Troki became the center of the Troki *uezd,* and some lands of Kovno *uezd* were added to this *uezd.*

14

Another new *guberniya* was established in 1866 when the Suvalki *guberniya* was created out of certain *uezds* taken from the Augustov *guberniya*.

The uezds

There have also been changes in *uezd* boundaries over the years. For example, in 1816 portion of Roseiny *uezd* was added to Kovno *uezd*. This means that in the earlier Lithuanian records, the towns of Ariogola, Babtai, Cekiski, Dotnuva, Grinkiskis, Josvainiai, Keidaniai, Krakes, Seredzius, Vandziogala and Vilkija would have been shown as part of Rosseiny *uezd*, whereas today they will be reflected as part of Kaunas *uezd*. Here again, the current archival allocation as reflected in Appendix A should be used.

Administration of the Jewish communities

In the Russia Empire everybody belonged to an estate or class (the nobility, clergy, urban dwellers or rural residents), and people of the same estate living in a locality formed an estate community. The elected superiors of each community dealt with communal matters such as the care of poor, old or disabled people of the community. An important function of the community was the collecting of taxes.

Until 1844 the Jewish population lived under a different regime; it was administered by Jewish administrative bodies, the *kahals*. These embraced all Jews in a given area, irrespective of their estates, and therefore did not fit into the estate system. In 1844 the *kahals* were abolished, and the administration of the Jewish population was taken over by local estate communities under the supervision of the *guberniya*. Some of the *kahals* were combined into new local communities, according to the population of the area. Out of the 119 former *kahals*, 74 such local communities were formed in 1844. A list showing the former *kahals* and the new Jewish communities can be found at www.jewishgen.org/litvak/vital-p4.htm. This turned out to be a significant development from the point of view of genealogical research, as the new local estate communities were now required to keep a whole batch of records, which now provide a valuable source of information for researchers (See page 33).

3

HOW TO GO ABOUT YOUR RESEARCH

The basic methodology of searching for your Lithuanian ancestors is

- first to identify one ancestor who lived there for at least portion of his life;

- then to determine whether his name appears anywhere in the available Lithuanian records; and finally

- to use any information you can gather about him in order to go further back in time, and look for any of *his* ancestors in older records. (The available records go back in some cases as far as 1764).

THE STARTING POINT: IDENTIFYING YOUR FIRST ANCESTOR

This may possibly be your father, but is more likely to be one of your two grandfathers, or even a great-grandfather. A male ancestor is likely to produce more results, as the old Lithuanian records have more details of males than of females, but if you have details of his wife also, that may be helpful.

The details you will need are

- the family name. Remember that the old records were kept in Russian, and that the way a name is spelt in a transliteration from the old records may not be exactly the same as you spell it today. The name your ancestor bore may also have changed since he lived in Lithuania, for a variety of possible reasons. (See Chapter 7 below for more information on names);

- your ancestor's first name, in its Hebrew or Yiddish form;

- the name of his father in its Hebrew or Yiddish form (helpful, but not essential); and

- the name of the town or *shtetl* in which your ancestor lived, and the district (*uezd*) in which it was located. This is an essential element in tracing your Lithuanian roots because the Lithuanian archival records that you will need to consult were kept on a local basis.

Your best source for finding these details will be your own family – anecdotal family history, old family papers, naturalization papers, passports, etc. Write or talk to your older family members. Ask them about family names, where they lived, when they immigrated, what town they came from. Look for old letters, certificates or photos (studio photos often indicate the photographer's address; notes may be written on the back).

Write, talk to, video or record every member of your family you can reach. Ask for family memorabilia, such as passports, photos and marriage certificates. Ask whether any members of the family went to settle in other countries. Find out where family members are buried (in the UK and elsewhere). Visit the cemeteries where possible and record the information on the tombstones.

Finding the *shtetl* name

In most cases, the name passed down in anecdotal family history will be the Yiddish name for the *shtetl*. Before you can consult the Lithuanian archival records for the *shtetl*, you will need to find the current Lithuanian name of the town. If you propose contacting the Lithuanian Archives directly and asking them to look up the records for you, they will in all probability know the present-day Lithuanian name for the town even if you give them the old Jewish name, but if you are going to do your own research in the lists now available on-line, you will need to find the current name yourself. A list of old *shtetl* names (in Yiddish and other languages) and their present-day Lithuanian equivalents will be found in Appendix A.

Some of the townlets in which our Lithuanian ancestors lived were very small, and the persons living there were registered in a larger neighbouring town. For example, Andreyev was the name of a very small settlement close to Rietavas. There was no separate Revision List for it, and its residents were included in the 1816 Revision List for Rietavas. A similar procedure was followed for the keepers of

17

country taverns; these were often situated on cross-roads, and although the location may have had a name of its own, the tavern-keeper and his family would have been regarded as part of the community of the nearest town. It is possible that the *shtetl* name which has come down to you through family sources is the name of such a smaller settlement, and that your ancestors were registered in the name of an adjoining town. If you cannot find a Revision List for the *shtetl* name known to you, you may need to think about looking for your family in the lists for a nearby town. To find such a town, you will need to consult a map of Lithuania, but first you will have to locate your own *shtetl* on the map. There are a number of ways of doing this. The online JewishGen programme ShtetlSeeker is at www.jewishgen.org/ShtetlSeeker. Enter the name of your *shtetl*, and it will give you the map co-ordinates for the town, as well as a link to an actual map which will show your *shtetl*. Another good online source is at http://earth-info.nga.mil/gns/html/index.html. Alternatively, you can use the search facility of Mapquest (www.mapquest.com); type in the name of the town and you will be given a map on which you can zoom in or out for varying degrees of detail. A very detailed on-line map of the Baltic States can also be found at www.virtual.lv.

The shtetl: A street in Rietavas, about 1900

If you decide to join one of the District Research Groups operating under the umbrella of the US-based LitvakSIG (see p. 48 below), you will also need to know the name of the district (*uezd*) in which your ancestral town is situated. That can also be ascertained from Appendix A. An on-line list of Lithuanian towns which is kept up-to-date is at www.jewishgen.org/Litvak/Shtetls/Lithuania.htm.

There are some instances, fortunately not many, where two or even more Lithuanian towns have the same name. There is, for example, a Kriukai in Siauliai *uezd* and another in Kaunas *uezd*. The Yiddish name for the former is Kruk, and for the latter Kruki, but the former was sometimes also known as Kruki. It would therefore be a good idea, when trying to find your ancestral *shtetl*, to check whether there is more than one town by that name by using the Mapquest search facility. If there are two or more towns with the same name, Mapquest will normally show all of them. To determine which of these is your ancestral *shtetl*, you will need to check the archival records of both towns to see if your family was included amongst its residents.

Confusion sometimes also arises between the name of the town and the name of the *guberniya* in which it was situated. When someone says their family was, for example, "from Kovno" or "from Vilna", they may be referring to the *guberniya*, and not to the particular town within the *guberniya* from which they came (just as someone who says he comes from "New York" is not necessarily from the city of New York; he may be referring to the state of New York, and his actual home town or city may be New York, or Albany, or any other town or city in the state).

Often a document will give a person's place of origin as "Russia" even though he came from what we now know as Lithuania. This is because the pre-WWI Czarist Russian Empire included the area that today constitutes Lithuania (as well as Latvia, Belarus, Ukraine and parts of Poland). There were comparatively few Jews who lived in the area that is actually within the boundaries of present-day Russia.

If you have been unable to find the name of your ancestral *shtetl* from family sources, you will need to look for a clue in public records such as naturalization records, shipping and passenger lists, or cemetery and burial records. There are many sources in the UK, the USA, South Africa and on the Internet from which you may be able to obtain clues to names of relatives, and to the names of the *shtetlach* from which they came. These sources are detailed in Chapter 9.

One such source is the **All Lithuania Database**, which is available online (www.jewishgen.org/Litvak/all.htm). This website contains information culled from a vast number of old Lithuanian records, and lists family names coupled with the name of the *shtetl* where the families were recorded as having been either resident or registered. The database includes a search engine that will enable you to search for all entries containing a particular family name. If you know the first name of your paternal grandfather, and that of his father, you may be able to identify him, and once you have done this, you will know the name of the *shtetl* where he lived or was registered. (For more on this database, see page 52 below).

Another database available on the Internet where you will probably be able to find persons with the same family name as yours is the **JewishGen Family Finder**. This is a database on which other researchers post notices asking for persons sharing their family name. They usually list the towns from which their ancestors came. Finding such a name will not automatically mean that your ancestors came from the same town; at most it will give you a lead to explore. If you write to the persons whose name you found, they may be able to help. The URL is www.jewishgen.org/jgff. (Illustration at page 47).

STEP TWO: FINDING YOUR ANCESTOR'S NAME IN THE LITHUANIAN RECORDS

Once you have determined the name of your ancestral *shtetl*, you can move on to the next step, which is to look for your ancestor's name in the old records kept by the Lithuanian archives. Whether the ancestor concerned is a grandfather or great-grandfather, the records containing his name will probably date back to the end of the 19th century or the early years of the 20th century. The records that may be helpful in this respect are detailed in Chapters 4 and 5.

STEP THREE: GOING FURTHER BACK IN TIME

Tracing your line of descent beyond your first Lithuanian ancestor may present some difficulty. Although a great many 19th century Lithuanians records have survived, many have been lost because of wars, fires, or other causes. The result is that in regard to some communities there are significant gaps, periods in time for which records are missing. It is therefore not unlikely, for example, that a researcher may find a reference to the family name in an 1816 revision list, but that the next available revision list for that town is that for 1858, where the family name again appears, but borne by different individuals. The problem is then to establish whether there is a link between the individuals who feature in the two lists and your first ancestor, or even between themselves. This may sometimes be comparatively easy, because most of the available records give the father's name for all individuals listed, and ages. In other cases, you may need to draw inferences from the Ashkenazi practice of naming children after a deceased grandparent. This means that where you have the same names appearing in two different generations, one of the persons bearing that name may be the grandson of the other. But it may not always be that easy to make a direct link between two records from different periods. It may be necessary to consult intermediate records of various types which relate to the same community, and combine the information from all of them to make the link. (cf. the Case Study in Chapter 11).

HOW IS ALL THIS TO BE ACHIEVED?

This may seem a daunting task, but there are various ways to approach it. One possible approach would be to ask the archivists at the various Lithuanian archives to do the research for you. Chapter 8 will show you how to contact them.   There are however some disadvantages in following this course.

- Firstly, depending upon which *guberniya* your ancestor lived in, the available records may be dispersed over different archives. Each of these archives contains entirely different records, no duplication is involved, and they operate independently. One is not a branch of the other. So you will need to determine which archive is likely to have the information you need, and you will then need to write to each archive separately, and pay a separate fee to each archive.

- Secondly, the archives have a large backlog of enquiries to deal with, and it may take you something like nine months to a year to get an answer.

- Thirdly, the information you receive will be limited to the particular family whose details you have requested.

Alternatively, you may engage a professional researcher living in Lithuania to do the research for you. If you follow this course, it is advisable to obtain references from previous clients, and that you have an agreement setting out exactly what is to be researched, the period to be covered by such research, and the contents of the report that you want the researcher to provide.

There is also a third alternative, one that has many advantages. Nowadays, because of the large number of databases accessible through your personal computer, it is possible to access the information contained in the Lithuanian archival records without going to Lithuania, or even approaching the various Lithuanian archives for assistance. This is speedier, cheaper, and may provide a great deal more information.

There is another point worth noting. A new law that came into force in Lithuania in January 2005 prevents the archives from giving out information from records that are less than 100 years old (the previous limit was 75 years), save for death records, where the limit is 50 years. But some of the databases accessible on the Internet may already have obtained information copied from records less than 100 years old, and they are not subject to this restriction.

Chapter 6 will tell you about these databases, and how to access them. But if you follow this route, you will first need to have an understanding of the various types of Lithuanian records that are available, and the information that each can provide. This is the subject of the next chapter.

4

TYPES OF RECORDS IN THE LITHUANIAN ARCHIVES

The records of Jewish interest housed in the Lithuanian archives are of many different kinds. For purposes of genealogical research they can be divided into three categories, according to the type or amount of information they provide:

- Records giving full family details;
- Records listing the household heads only;
- Vital records.

RECORDS GIVING FULL FAMILY DETAILS

These are the most fruitful sources of information for anybody researching family roots. This is because they list households, and provide details of all the members of the household, which means that you can expand your family tree horizontally for each generation as well as vertically. On these lists, one would normally find the surname of the family, the first name of the father, the names of each family member residing in the household, the age of each person in the year when the list was created, and the relationship of each person to the head of the household (these relationships include wife, son, daughter, sister, grandchild, daughter-in-law, nephew, niece, cousin's wife, cousin's child, etc). The lists may also show other families living in the same household. The families may or may not be related; sometimes more than one family may simply have lived in the same building. (See the extract on page 49 below).

The typical example of such a list would be a census return, but for the territory with which we are concerned, the lists in this category varied in type from time to time and went by different names. The different types are listed below.

The All Russia Census of 1895-7

As explained in Chapter 3, the search for your immediate ancestor will probably need to start in the records created about the end of the 19th century or the beginning of the 20th century. The most useful of these would normally have been the All Russia Census of 1895-7. This was the first and only true census of the population of the Czarist Russian Empire The entire population, men, women and children, were listed according to place of residence regardless of where they were officially registered. The census was conducted on a household basis, and included the address where the family lived, where they were registered, where each member was born, the name of his or her father, and his or her age and occupation.

Unfortunately, pursuant to a resolution of the Czarist government, the lists were destroyed after the census calculations were completed and statistics gathered, and it is only by accident that some portions survived. Only about 10% of the portion relating to Lithuania still exists in the State Historical Archives in Vilnius, although it is possible that some additional portions for Lithuania are stored in the

Moscow and/or St. Petersburg archives. The table below shows the percentage of the census that has survived, in so far as it relates to Jewish inhabitants.

In 1999–2000 Howard Margol and Peggy Freedman collected and co-ordinated the data relating to these areas and had them translated. These have now been put into a database and published on a special website which is searchable by name, place, soundex value and keyword. More information, including an index of the towns that are included together with the number of families listed for each town, can be found on the website. See page 54.

Uezd / District	Gubernia	% Remaining	No of families
Kaunas	Kovno	0%	0
Ukmerge	Kovno	14%	834
Zarasai	Kovno	14%	637
Panevezys	Kovno	5%	251
Raseniai	Kovno	4%	194
Telsiai	Kovno	3%	82
Siauliai	Kovno	2%	200
Vilnius (not including city of Vilna)	Vilna	18%	316

Surviving portions of the 1895-7 All Russia census

The entire translation of the existing Jewish records from this census was donated to the Family History Library in Salt Lake City, Utah, which has re-produced them on microfiche. The title on the microfiche is "1897 census extracts from Lithuania". The Family History Library Catalogue (FHLC) description is: "Filming: 459 exposures on 10 microfiches (105 mm.), GS6001828". A copy of the microfiche can be ordered through your local LDS Family History Center (ordering number: 6,001,828). (See page 80).

If you are lucky enough to find that the 1897 census records relating to your ancestral *shtetl* have survived, you will find a great deal of helpful information there.

Military Lists

If the portions of the 1895-7 census relating to your ancestral *shtetl* have not survived, you may find material relating to the early 20th century in a military list. These were lists either of draftees (men who were scheduled to be drafted that year for military service), or of those who did not turn up for military service. In both types of list, the entire family of the conscript was listed as a standard practice because fines were imposed on the family of men who did not turn up for military service. The Kaunas archives have a list for the entire district of Raseiniai of men who avoided conscription in 1912, and a further list of family members for 1914. (This was prior to the onset of World War I). The number of families listed for each town in the district is relatively small, but in respect of those families, the lists are a possible alternative to the 1897 census as a starting point for your research.

Czarist Revision Lists ("Revizskaia Skaska")

For the period prior to 1860, full family details are provided by the so-called "revision lists" drawn up by the Czarist authorities. These lists were instituted in 1719 when a national poll tax was introduced, changing the basis of taxation from households to individuals, and subsequent lists were taken periodically. The first list was started in 1719, and a lengthy period often elapsed between each revision. A total of ten principal Revision Lists were made in Russia up to 1860, but only five of these were made after the incorporation of Lithuania into the Russian empire.

1811-1812	6th Revision List
1816-1826	7th Revision List
1833-1836	8th Revision List
1850-1853	9th Revision List
1857-1860	10th Revision List

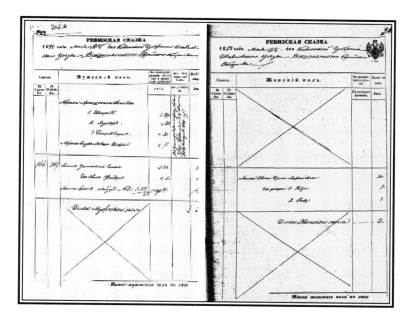

Two facing pages from the 1858 Revision List for Leckava. The left-hand page contains details of the male members of the household, while the right-hand page lists the female members of the household.

The records were written in Russian (Cyrillic) except for the 1811 list, which was in Polish.

Although a revision list was akin to a census in some respects, it served a different purpose. Its main objectives were to obtain a list of tax-payers and a list for conscription purposes. The actual translation of the Russian name (*Revizskaia Skaska*) is something like "Inspection Reports". The term "revision lists" probably derives from the fact that, unlike the Western form of census, the lists were revised or updated, sometimes several times, in the period that elapsed before the next list was drawn up. The last three revision lists also noted what had happened to people registered on the list since the last revision list, or where they previously lived, so the information on a list may cover a period of ten years or more.

In the periods between the principal revision lists, Supplemental (or Additional) Revision Lists were drawn up to provide information about families who for some reason had not been included in the principal lists.

The revision list recorded all residents belonging to the class of taxpayers. The entire family was listed, with their ages, father's name, and other useful details. Information was provided about what had happened to every person since the last revision: who had died, who was conscripted, who moved, who came to town, and when he came. All relationships to the head of the household were made clear. Revision Lists recorded Jews according to the place where they were registered, not where they resided. For example: a family may have always lived in Kovno but be officially registered in Kelme; it would then be listed on the Kelme revision list and not on the Kovno revision list.

Bear in mind that the lists are not wholly reliable. Because they were used for conscription purposes, the Jewish inhabitants often provided false information about their families. If there were two sons named Chaim and Josel, they might register one only and give his name as Chaim Josel. Or, because of the rule that where a family had only one son, he was exempt from military duty, a father with two sons would sometimes register one as the son of his brother or sister.

Most of the surviving revision lists are stored in the State Historical Archives in Vilnius, although there are a few odd portions in the Kaunas Regional Archives. The most complete collection of revision lists is that relating to Vilna *guberniya*. The collection for Kovno *guberniya* is rather small, and consists mainly of supplemental revision lists. Only a small number of principal revision lists for Kovno *guberniya* survived: these are for Ukmerge (previously Vilkomir) *uezd*, Siauliai *uezd* and Raseiniai *uezd*, all for the year 1858.

Family Lists

Amongst the new records which the local community authorities were required to keep when they replaced the Jewish *kahals* in 1844, were family lists. These were much the same as the revision lists, in that they also recorded the names and details of all members of the household, and their relationship to the head of the household, although a family list usually contained somewhat more information than a revision list. For example, it would list the occupation of the householder. In some sources you will find both types of documents referred to as censuses, but technically they were different. While revision lists are stored in the Lithuanian State Historical Archives in Vilnius, family lists for towns in Kovno *guberniya* are stored in the Kaunas Regional Archives. For more about these lists, see the comments by Vitalija Gircyte at www.jewishgen.org/Litvak/vitalija-writes.htm.

For a period of time, there was an overlap: some areas had family lists as early as 1847, while others still produced revision lists, but after 1860 the revision lists ceased and were effectively replaced by the family lists. There were family lists for 1874, 1887, 1890 and 1908. In 1874, all of the Jewish population of Kovno *guberniya* was listed in family lists. The Kaunas Regional Archive has most of these for the Kovno *uezd*.

District Merchants Lists

These are lists of the merchants (of 1st, 2nd and 3rd classes) who were permitted to trade in the *uezd*, and often included details of the entire family, their relationship to the head of the household, and ages. These lists are an important supplementary source of information because merchants were frequently not listed in general family or tax-payer lists.

Jews living in rural areas of the *uezd*

This is another type of list, kept on a district basis, that fills a gap for a period for which there are no surviving revision or family lists.

Prior to 1795: Censuses of the Grand Duchy of Lithuania

The area now known as Lithuania was not always part of Czarist Russia. Prior to 1795, before it was annexed to Czarist Russia as part of the third and final partition of Poland, and when it was still part of the Grand Duchy of Lithuania ("GDL"), there were censuses undertaken. There were Jewish censuses taken in the Grand Duchy as early as 1650 and 1662, but the earliest censuses still extant in the Lithuania State Historical Archives were those made in 1765 and 1784. As in the case of all Polish records, these censuses were in Latin script.

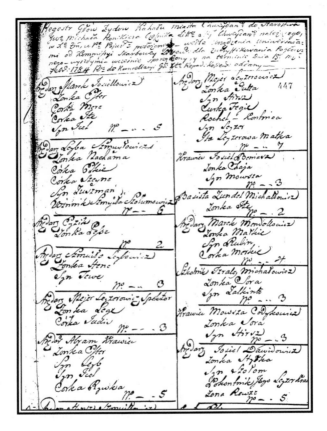

A page from the 1784 GDL Census

There is a major difficulty in using these censuses for genealogical purposes: Jewish families were not required to adopt surnames until 1804, so the entries are in most cases in the form of patronymics (names formed from the father's name, e.g., Hirsh Shimonowicz, the Polish for Hirsh the son of Shimon). The only way of attributing surnames to the families recorded in these censuses is to find a link between them and the families listed in a later Czarist Revision List

30

(1811 or 1816), by which time surnames had been adopted. To find such a link one needs to look for a combination of names in the GDL census (e.g. two men with the same patronymic, who may therefore be brothers), and then try to find matching names (two men with the same name, and the same father) in a later revision list.

I can illustrate this by an example from my own family researches.

- The 1784 GDL list for Kvedarna lists two men with the same patronymic: Hyrsz Szmujllowicz and Lejba Szmujllowicz. The patronymic is the Polish form for "son of Szmujllo". They were probably brothers, but this cannot be asserted with certainty by simply looking at this one list. Hyrsz is shown as having a son named Szmujllo, aged 4, which means he was born about 1780.
- The 1816 Czarist revision list for Kvedarna lists two persons named Shmuel ben Hirsh Aron (born 1780) and Shmuel ben Leib Aron (born 1763).

There is a clear connection to the 1784 GDL list in that the first of the two persons mentioned in the 1816 list, Shmuel ben Hirsh Aron, is obviously Szmujllo, the son of Hyrsz Szmujllowicz, who was mentioned in the 1784 list. The second person mentioned, Shmuel ben Leib Aron, appears to be his cousin, a son of Lejba Szmujllowicz, and named after a common grandfather, but there is a question mark about this because this Shmuel's name does not appear in the 1784 list as a son in Lejba's household. However a closer examination of the material resolves this problem. According to the 1816 list Shmuel ben Leib was born in 1763, which suggests that he was probably already married and living in his own home when the 1784 census was taken. Another look at the 1784 census confirms this: it shows a separate entry for the household of a Szmujllo Lejbowicz (the patronymic for "son of Lejbe"). Moreover, the name of his wife as given there is the same as that of the wife of Shmuel ben Leib Aron in the 1816 census.

This confirms that the Hyrsz and Lejba Szmujllowicz whose names appear on the 1784 GDL census were indeed brothers (the sons of Szmujllo), and were the fathers respectively of the two Aron cousins

31

whose names appear on the 1816 revision list, and that the surname Aron was adopted by the family sometime between 1784 and 1816.

The difficulty in identifying persons listed in these early GDL documents is compounded by the fact that some of the lists are for large areas whose boundaries did not coincide with those of the *uezds* in later years. For example, the Raseiniai District Research Group has acquired a copy of the 1764 Register of the Jubarkas Kahal. It contains the patronymics of 2,282 persons. For 1,663 of these, the towns in which they lived are given. There were 12 of these towns, some in Rosseiny *uezd*, some in Suvalki *uezd*, and some in Kudirkos Naumiestis *uezd,* which shows that the Jubarkas Kahal had jurisdiction over a very large area. While it might be possible to identify those persons whose places of residence are given, for the remaining 619 persons we have only patronymics, and given the wide territory covered by the Register, it will be virtually impossible to link them with names appearing in a later Czarist list.

The first translations of the GDL censuses in the Vilnius archives were acquired by David and Sonia Hoffmann, who are now concentrating their research on these early GDL records. To further this research they have established the Jewish Family History Foundation. (See page 54). The two GDL censuses contain records relating to 138 towns in the area of the present-day Lithuania. The names of these towns can be found on the Foundation's website at www.jewishfamilyhistory.org. The Foundation has indicated that as and when each *kahal* list on these GDL censuses is funded and transliterated, they will be published on its website.

RECORDS LISTING HOUSEHOLD HEADS ONLY

This is the second of our three categories of archival records. Records in this group show only the heads of households, sometimes with the names of their fathers and their ages, but rarely with any further information. (See the extract at page 50 below). They have some usefulness in tracing your ancestry, but this is limited. They can confirm the existence of the individuals named therein, and where they lived, and by giving the age of the individual, and the name of his father, they can often help a researcher establish a vertical line of descent. It is also often possible to identify a brother by the name of a common father. What these lists lack are details of female ancestors, and of children.

The lists which are available generally date from shortly after 1844, when local community administrations replaced the Jewish *kahals* and were required to keep various lists. They included lists such as Box and Candle Tax Lists, Lists of People Unable to Pay their Taxes, Voters Lists, Real Estate Owners Lists, Lists of Farmers, and of Tavern Keepers, and so on. The archives also have other types of records, that is to say, in addition to those which the municipal authorities were required to keep, such as Postal Savings Bank Records and Passport Registration Books. Apart from the Family Lists, these lists did not contain as much detail as the revision lists. Descriptions follow of some of those more frequently found.

Box Tax Lists

The first recorded Box Tax dates back to 1647, but the tax lists that are presently available relate to the tax regulated by Russian decrees of 1839 and 1844. This tax was levied on animals and poultry ritually slaughtered, and again on every pound of kosher meat sold in the Jewish community. It was also levied on supplementary items such as the rental profits of Jewish-owned property, and for wearing ritual items of clothing. It was used to support the local municipality, for charity purposes, to pay the taxes for poor Jews, and part of it went to various government purposes. For a full history of the tax and a description of how it worked see the paper by Anatolij Chayesh at www.jewishgen.org/litvak/BoxTaxPaperwork.htm.

The tax was levied on the community as a whole, but lists were kept of individual members of the community who contributed and those who were too indigent to do so. It is these lists which are of genealogical interest as they give the name of the family, the first name of the head of each household in the community, and his father's name. Sometimes the number of family members, occupation, and financial status are indicated. It is however rare for other members of the household to be listed.

Box tax records are also of wider interest as they include records dealing with the financial position of individual communities, and often petitions by particular communities for money to be provided for specific purposes. Many interesting examples are given by Anatolij Chayesh in the paper referred to above.

Candle Tax Lists

The Candle Tax was a tax on the sale of Shabbos candles. The money raised through the tax was applied for the needs of Jewish education. Most Candle Tax payers lists state the name of the taxpayer, his father's name, the number of males and females in the household but not their names, and the amount of tax paid. Occasionally, a Candle Tax list will also include the age of the taxpayer and the name of his wife.

Lists exist for almost all Jewish communities in Kovno *guberniya*. Most of the surviving lists are for 1846, 1877, 1892, and 1904, and for some communities for 1908 and 1912. Very few details were given. The list of taxpayers was usually broken down by "well-to-do families," "average families," and "poor families."

People unable to pay their taxes

These lists give the names of the household heads only, but in respect of these they record the names of their fathers and their ages. They can therefore sometimes be very useful in tracing a lineage further back into time. They also provide colourful information as to why the person listed was unable to pay their taxes: either they had died, or were ill, or blind, or had been recruited, and so on.

Voters lists

These were of various kinds

Rabbi's Electors List: - This was a list of the permanent town dwellers who had a right to participate in the election of the Rabbi. This list usually includes the family name of the eligible voter, the first name and father's name or patronymic, and often the age of the voter.

List of Electors of Representatives to Local Municipalities - This is similar to the rabbi's electors lists.

Real Estate Owners List

There are many kinds of real estate owner's lists, with varying amounts of information. Some are quite detailed, noting the documentation that proves ownership, exactly what was owned and how the property was used, as well as any charges against the property, the value of the property, and a full listing of the entire family living on the property. Some give only the surname and name of the owner. Within this category of files are lists of Jews "who illegally owned property belonging to Christians."

The Kaunas archives has town plans (*plat* maps) of a number of *shtetlach* drawn up in about 1910, showing lot numbers. These can sometimes be correlated with the lot numbers appearing on the lists of real estate owners, enabling you to locate exactly where your family lived. The Historical Archives in Vilnius has a number of town plans drawn up in the previous century. Two examples are the 1863 town plan for Linkuva and the 1865 town plan for Pusalotas. Both include a list of property owners which can be correlated with the lot-numbers on the town plans.

Postal Savings Records

These records date from about 1890, when the use of the postal savings bank became popular, and run through to about 1915. The records are quite informative because the depositor was required to complete a form giving details which included father's name, age or date of birth, places of birth and residence, occupation, and in the case of a female depositor, her maiden name.

Internal Passports

There are two types of internal passports amongst the records: those issued to Russian travellers prior to World War I, and the documents known by the same name and issued to citizens of the new state of Lithuania established at the end of that war. There is a major difference between the two types. Prior to 1918, all Russian citizens traveling within the boundaries of Russia, whether Jewish or not, were required to have an internal passport. These were issued by local municipalities, town dwellers administration, or the police. Some records of the issuance of these passport books have survived. They exist only for a few Jewish communities, and for only some years, although there are many issuance records for Kovno *uezd* for 1874-75. They give details of the family members, the name of each person's father, ages, and a physical description of each person.

After World War I, when Lithuania became an independent country, every Lithuanian citizen over the age of 17 was required to carry an internal passport. The significant feature of these passports was that they were intended to serve not as travel documents, but as personal identification documents. They also gave Lithuanian citizenship, and after about 1922 anybody without one could be sent back to the USSR. Applicants had to prove the right to Lithuanian citizenship by producing evidence that they were residents of the territory of Lithuania before World War I.

The Lithuanian internal passport itself contained basic information such as name, surname, date of birth, place of birth, address, nationality, religion, and occupation. The supporting files are more informative; they contain all the information that the applicants would have needed to prove that either they or their parents were born or had lived in the region of Lithuania before World War I, including copies of birth and marriage certificates, affidavits, etc, as well as photographs. They are accordingly an important source of genealogical information. Unfortunately access to these passports may be limited by a new law that came into force in January 2005, limiting access to documents less than 100 years old. For more information about these Internal Passports, see page 55 below, and at www.jewishgen.org/databases/Lithuania/InternalPassports.htm

Prenumeranten Lists

These were lists of subscribers for Rabbinic books from 1835 to 1913. For a list of communities for which these prenumeranten lists exist, see Berl Kagan: *Hebrew Subscription Lists* (New York, 1975).   As to the abbreviation of names used in these lists, see the article at www.jewishgen.org/Litvak/prenum.htm by Ed Cohler.

LISTS FROM ARCHIVES OUTSIDE LITHUANIA

Occasionally lists are found in the archives of other countries which relate directly to areas in present-day Lithuania. The following are examples of these:

Family list of Kovno *guberniya* Jews expelled from Riga

This is an 1895 list of the heads of households of Jewish families from Kovno *guberniya* who had moved to Riga and had been legally adopted by Riga Jewish families and, as adopted sons, were registered as belonging to Riga Jewish community. When this became known after complaints by some other Riga Jews, the Senate of Russia (at that time the highest court) decided that adopted sons did not have the right automatically to become members of the Riga Jewish community. The adoptions were cancelled and the families were required to return to their previous places of residence. This list is taken from a file of correspondence, and there are a few papers on each family.

Riga passport list

People leaving the Pale were required to register their internal passports with the police (see page 35). The JewishGen LatviaSIG has obtained a list of people who registered in Riga in 1900 which consists largely of people living in Lithuania. The names are on the All Latvia Database :   www.jewishgen.org/databases/Latvia.

Lida *uezd*

Lida *uezd* was at one time in Grodno *guberniya*. Most of it is now located in modern day Belarus, with only a small part remaining in Lithuania. Consequently there are many records relating to towns in the Lida district in the Grodno archive in Belarus. These include records for Lida, Oshmiani and Vileiki (Naujoji Vilnia). See the list at www.shtetlinks.jewishgen.org/Lida-District/grod-arch.htm.

Polish "Aliyah Passports"

In the 1930s several thousand Polish Jews managed to emigrate to what was then Palestine. They were required, upon receiving identity documents in their new homeland, to turn in their Polish passports to the Polish Consulate at their destination and the invalidated Polish passports were returned to the Foreign Ministry in Warsaw. The Polish Government has since given these "Palestine passports" to the Jewish Historical Institute in Warsaw to preserve as historical documents. The collection spans the years 1929 to 1939 and consists of 3,754 Polish passports.

Because Vilna and adjacent areas formed part of Poland in the inter-war years, the collection includes passports issued to residents of towns such Vilna and Eisiskis which are now in Lithuania

These passports include date and place of birth, last place of residence, occupation and civil status (single, married, etc.). Details of children appear in some instances. The various official stamps and seals that appear inside trace the entire route taken by the emigrant and (on occasion) onward travels to other countries, providing precise dates for each leg of the journey.

A full account, including an alphabetical list of the places of birth of passport holders, is available on the website of the Jewish Records Indexing project at www.jewishgen.org/JRI-PL/jhi/jri-jhi-aliyah-passport.htm.

VITAL RECORDS

These constitute the last of our three categories of documents in the Lithuanian archives. Vital records (records of births, marriages, and deaths) would normally be amongst the records one would want to see when researching one's ancestry, but although these may provide useful additional information to fill in the details when one has already identified ancestors, and knows when they were born, married or died, as the case may be, they are of limited direct help in tracing ancestors who have not yet been identified. Their main usefulness lies in ascertaining the names of parents, and possibly, the places of birth, which may indicate how members of the family moved about.

Metric books (vital records) were introduced in the Russian Empire in 1835. The Regulation on Jews of April 1835 required the rabbi of each community to keep a register of births, marriages, divorces and deaths in the community. The first books were started in 1837. Jews were required to register the life cycle events at the synagogue to which they were assigned, and each year the government authorities went to the synagogues to copy these registers. The records were written in Russian (and in the Cyrillic alphabet). Some, but not all records were then duplicated in Hebrew or Yiddish. In Suvalki *guberniya*, the procedure was slightly different from that in Kovno and Vilna *gubernii*: the life cycle event was first recorded in the synagogue, but the record was then copied and recorded at the Civil Office, either in Polish or Russian.

Practically all the original synagogue records were destroyed in 1941, when the Germans invaded Russia. There are some exceptions: for example, nine books of Jewish vital records covering the period from 1925-1940 are known to have survived in Panevezys. In other cases the only surviving records are the copies stored in the archives.

Unfortunately, even in the case of archival copies of vital records only bits and pieces of the 19th and early 20th century records have survived. Originally, they were not all stored in the same archives, but in 2000 the archival system was re-organized, and all vital record books prior to 1915 are now centralized in the Lithuanian State Historical Archive in Vilnius. Vital records after 1940 are kept in the Lithuanian Central Civil Register Archives, also in Vilnius.

The Kaunas Regional Archive has no original vital records, but has a few isolated copies and abstracts. It has abstracts of birth records for Rokiskis, which were used to prove identity, and of birth records for

Kovno for 1904 and 1915; for Jonava for 1851-1864; and for Krakes 1896-1912; late 19th century copies of marriage certificates in Kovno, and abstracts of marriages for Rokiskis; and of death records for Rokiskis. Some copies exist as part of a file pertaining to other matters, i.e., a passport application, a legal proceeding, etc. Finding these vital records would be accidental as they are not filed separately.

Some of the vital record book of Jewish communities of the old Suvalki *guberniya* are now stored in the archives of Suwalki, Poland.

Vital records in the Family History Library

The Church of the Latter Day Saints (Mormons) embarked on a project between January 2000 and October 2002 to microfilm the vital records at the Lithuanian State Historical Archives, in Vilnius (LVIA). Their Family History Library at Salt Lake City now has microfilms of vital records for a large number of Lithuanian towns (microfilm numbers 2,157,888 through 2,343,143) (229 reels). The Library references are:

- Vilna *guberniya* crown rabbinate metrical records, 1837-1925 (132 reels) LVIA Fond 728 (series 1, files 1-1127; series 2, files 1-406; series 3, files 1-1560; series 4, files 1-474);
- Kovno *guberniya* crown rabbinate metrical records (93 reels) LVIA Fond 1226 (series 1, files 1-2177; series 2, files 1-202);
- Suvalki *guberniya* metrical books (4 reels) LVIA Fond 1108: (series 1, files 1-38).

The microfilms are available for borrowing at any local LDS Family History Centre. A locality index prepared by Kahlile Mehr of the FHL makes it easier to find the microfilm ordering numbers for the specific place, date, and event type you need.

The JewishGen LitvakSIG has begun to index the metrical registers contained within the FHL microfilms. The LitvakSIG came to an agreement with the Mormons and the Lithuanian Archives to have the FHL supply the SIG a set of digital images of the entire set of vital records. In return, the LitvakSIG has indexed the records and shares these indexes with both the Lithuanian Archives and the FHL.

40

The microfilms so far obtained are for over 100 towns in the Vilna, Kovno, and Suvalki *gubernii*. The list of towns is available online at www.jewishgen.org/databases/FHLC/VilnaMicrofilmsIndex.htm

Records for many towns cover the time period from 1850-1914; others have records from 1890-1915. There are often missing years in a series. The vital records for the city of Vilna span the years 1837-1915 inclusive. This project contains roughly 500,000 records. Not all these records have yet been indexed. This is an on-going project. Although records for several towns have already been indexed, no one town has had all its records completely indexed, proofed, and submitted to the All Lithuania Database (ALDB) (see below, page 52). As indexes are completed and proofed, the details are submitted for inclusion in the ALDB. If you want to see the complete index for any particular town, you will need to become a member of the Project. Membership in the Vital Records Project is on a town-by-town basis. A $100 contribution is required to join for each town. In order to join the project for a given town, go to the LitvakSIG web page at www.jewishgen.org/litvak.

Further reading

The website of the Miriam Weiner Routes to Roots Foundation, Inc. (www.rtrfoundation.org) provides more information about the categories of material available in the various Lithuanian archives. It carries the following articles on the subject:

Laima Tautvaisaite: *An Overview of Lithuanian Archives, with a focus on the Lithuanian State Historical Archives.*

Galina Baranova: *A Selected Overview of Documents in the Lithuanian State Historical Archives Pertaining to Jewish Institutions/Organizations.* (See also her article at www.jewishgen.org/Litvak/Galina.htm).

Vitalija Gircyte: *Kaunas Regional Archives*

Dalius Zizys: *Lithuania Central State Archives*

41

5

WHAT RECORDS ARE AVAILABLE FOR YOUR SHTETL?

Tracing one's roots is often a bit like putting together the pieces of a jigsaw puzzle, but for those seeking to trace their Lithuanian antecedents back into the 19th century, there is an added complication: frequently pieces of the puzzle are missing. There were at one time many 19th century records relating to the Jewish community in existence which gave a substantial amount of family detail, but many of these were destroyed (wholly or partially), either in wartime or during pogroms, or by the fires that used to plague some of the communities. During World War I much archival material was evacuated to Russia and scattered there, and some of it was destroyed in 1914-1915, although in 1920 the newly established Lithuanian state managed to recover part of the evacuated archive material from Soviet Russia. There were further disruptions during World War II: some archive documents were transported to the USSR or Germany, and some of these were destroyed.

Despite all this, a large number of records have survived, and from time to time new batches of documents are even now being discovered in one or other archive. What records, then, can you expect to find for your *shtetl*?

The answer will depend largely upon which *guberniya* your ancestral *shtetl* was in. Some generalizations are possible. In broad terms:

- If your *shtetl* was in Vilna *guberniya*, a number of Czarist revision lists for your *shtetl* covering the period from 1811 to 1860 and some family lists covering the period from about 1850 to 1908 are likely to be available for research purposes.

However there are not yet any community lists such as box tax lists, candle tax lists, voters lists, etc, available. According to Galina Baranova, the Head Archivist at the Lithuanian State Historical Archives (LVIA) in Vilnius, this is not because they do not exist (they very probably do), but because the Jewish records in the archives would be included amongst some 16 km of documents relating to a number of religious groups in all three of the former *gubernii*, and the archivists simply have not had the time or resources available to check through this vast collection. They have in the main been able to answer queries from researchers by referring to the revision and family lists only. This suggests that despite the lack of the community lists, the chances of your being able to trace your ancestry back as far as 1811 on the basis of information in the revision and family lists are reasonably good.

There should also be various types of vital records available for your *shtetl*.

If your *shtetl* was in that portion of Vilna *guberniya* which was occupied by Poland from 1918-1940, there may be records for that period in the Polish archives.

- If your *shtetl* was in Kovno *guberniya*, the situation is reversed. There are not likely to be any revision lists for it other than for 1816 and perhaps 1858, but there will probably be a family list for 1874, and there may be other family lists for later years. It is therefore highly unlikely that you will be able to do a full trace of your ancestry from revision and family lists alone.

Fortunately the various types of community lists for Kovno *guberniya* covering the period from 1844 to about 1912, as well as some military lists, were kept in the Kaunas Regional Archives rather than in Vilnius, and as these are in a comparatively small repository, Vitalija Gircyte, the Chief Archivist at this institution, has been able to make these available for research. By using these it may well be possible for you to plug the gaps in the revision lists. (See the Case Study in Chapter 11 for an example).

Some vital records for your *shtetl* may also have survived. These would be in the LVIA.

- If your *shtetl* was in Suvalki *guberniya*, there are no 19th century revision lists available, but there are some tax lists in the Warsaw archives. There are probably community records at the LVIA in Vilnius, but the position is as described for towns in Vilna *guberniya*. Tracing your ancestry will be difficult. There may also be some documents in the Polish State Archives in Warsaw and Suwalki.

  In 1994 the LVIA began a detailed study of the material from Suvalki *guberniya* in those archives. See the article by Galina Baranova, *A Selected Overview of Documents in the Lithuanian State Historical Archives Pertaining to Jewish Institutions/Organizations,* published on the Routes to Roots Foundation website at www.rtrfoundation.org. See also another article by her published on the JewishGen website at www.jewishgen.org/Litvak/Galina.htm, and also the website at www.jewishgen.org/SuwalkLomza

Finding put what records are available

The results for no two *shtetlach* will be exactly the same. How do you find out what materials are available for your particular *shtetl?*

If you join one of the District Research Groups (see page 48 below), you will immediately gain access via e-mail to most of the information currently available for your *shtetl*. Not necessarily *all* the material, because as described in Chapter 6, the Groups are engaged in an on-going task of having the material translated. If you do not choose to join such a group, or if there is not group for your particular *uezd,* you will need to consult one of the published catalogues.

Because of the various disruptions described at the beginning of this chapter, there was until some years ago no comprehensive detailed catalogue of what records exist. But with the growing number of genealogical enquiries from Jewish researchers since approximately the 1990s, various attempts have been made to catalogue the materials of Jewish interest. Today it is fairly easy, by going on-line, to find more precise details of what records are available for each *shtetl*.

- An extremely useful on-line aid, covering all areas of Lithuania (as well as other countries in Eastern Europe), is the Routes to Roots website at www.rtrfoundation.org.

  It carries a searchable database of all the records available in the various Lithuanian archives for each town.

Routes to Roots Foundation, Inc.

SEARCH DATABASE

12 Record groups are available for the locality / town of: **SIAULIAI**.

To see detailed information, click on the entry of interest under "Document Type"

Country	Apskrit / District	Repository City	Document Type	Archive Type
LITHUANIA	SIAULIAI	KAUNAS	ARMY/RECRUITS	ARCHIVES
LITHUANIA	SIAULIAI	VILNIUS	BIRTH	ARCHIVES
LITHUANIA	SIAULIAI	KAUNAS	CENSUS	ARCHIVES
LITHUANIA	SIAULIAI	VILNIUS	CENSUS	ARCHIVES
LITHUANIA	SIAULIAI	VILNIUS	DEATH	ARCHIVES
LITHUANIA	SIAULIAI	KAUNAS	VOTER LISTS	ARCHIVES
LITHUANIA	SIAULIAI	VILNIUS2	KAHAL/JEWISH COM	ARCHIVES
LITHUANIA	SIAULIAI	KAUNAS	PROPERTY OWNERS	ARCHIVES
LITHUANIA	SIAULIAI	VILNIUS	MARRIAGE	ARCHIVES
LITHUANIA	SIAULIAI	KAUNAS	TAX LIST	ARCHIVES
LITHUANIA	SIAULIAI	VILNIUS	DIVORCE	ARCHIVES
LITHUANIA	SIAULIAI	KAUNAS	LOCAL GOVERNMENT	ARCHIVES

ARCHIVE
ACKNOWLEDGMENTS
ARCHIVE CHAPTERS
ARCHIVE DATABASE
MAPS
FOUNDATION DATA
PUBLICATIONS
RELATED WEBSITES
SUPPORTERS

Home

Result of searching the Routes to Roots website for records relating to the town of Siauliai. Each record group can be separately searched.

The Miriam Weiner
Routes to Roots Foundation, Inc. | **ARCHIVE DATABASE**

INTRODUCTION
ARCHIVE ACKNOWLEDGMENTS
ARCHIVE CHAPTERS
ARCHIVE DATABASE
MAPS
FOUNDATION DATA
PUBLICATIONS
RELATED WEBSITES
SUPPORTERS

Home

Locality/Town	:	SIAULIAI
Rajon/Region	:	SIAULIAI
Apskrit/District	:	SIAULIAI
Country	:	LITHUANIA
Archive Name	:	KAUNAS REGIONAL ARCHIVES
Archive Locale	:	KAUNAS
Archive Type	:	ARCHIVES
Document Type	:	TAX LIST
Year List	:	1846; 1877; 1908; 1912-1915; 1913
Fond/Opis/Delo	:	49/1/1381, 12938, 26862; 402/1/5; 106/1/475
See Also	:	
D-M Soundex	:	480000

**Click here for the address of the archive listed above
and additional important information for towns in LITHUANIA**

Guide to Administrative Districts by Country

RTR Foundation home page > Archive Database

*Stage 2 of an RTR search for Siauliai records: the result of clicking
on the Tax List link.*

- The All-Lithuania Database (see page 52) does not specifically give a list of what records are available for your *shtetl*, but it contains extracts from almost all the available lists. By entering your *shtetl* name in the search facility, and then working through the available records, you can determine what records have been used.

- In 1999 the LitvakSIG published an on-line catalogue of the Jewish materials in the Kaunas archive prepared by the chief archivist Vitalija Gircyte. It lists the towns in Kaunas *guberniya* alphabetically, and catalogues all the materials in that archive in respect of each such town. Because of the length of the list, it is spread over a number of web-pages. Go to www.jewishgen.org/litvak/kaunas0.htm, to find the list for towns starting with the letters from A-J. Links at the top of the page will take you to the web-pages for the towns from K-Z. The list was updated in August 2004.

If you do not have an on-line facility, you can consult *Jewish Vital Records, Revision Lists and other Jewish Holdings in the Lithuanian Archives*, a monograph published in 1996 by Harold Rhode and Sallyann Amdur Sack, which catalogued the types of records available for each *shtetl*. It is comprehensive as far as vital records are concerned, but not as complete on other types of records.

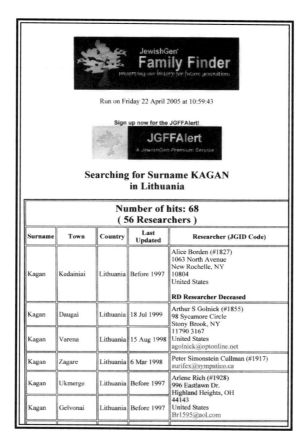

JewishGen
Family Finder
presenting our history for future generations

Run on Friday 22 April 2005 at 10:59:43

Sign up now for the JGFFAlert!

JGFFAlert
A JewishGen Premium Service

**Searching for Surname KAGAN
in Lithuania**

**Number of hits: 68
(56 Researchers)**

Surname	Town	Country	Last Updated	Researcher (JGID Code)
Kagan	Kedainiai	Lithuania	Before 1997	Alice Borden (#1827) 1063 North Avenue New Rochelle, NY 10804 United States **RD Researcher Deceased**
Kagan	Daugai	Lithuania	18 Jul 1999	Arthur S Golnick (#1855) 98 Sycamore Circle Stony Brook, NY 11790 3167
Kagan	Varena	Lithuania	15 Aug 1998	United States agolnick@optonline.net
Kagan	Zagare	Lithuania	6 Mar 1998	Peter Simonstein Cullman (#1917) aurifex@sympatico.ca
Kagan	Ukmerge	Lithuania	Before 1997	Arlene Rich (#1928) 996 Eastlawn Dr. Highland Heights, OH 44143
Kagan	Gelvonai	Lithuania	Before 1997	United States Brl595@aol.com

The first of six pages on the JewishGen Family Finder website listing persons searching for ancestors named Kagan (see page 78)

47

6

ACCESSING LITHUANIAN DATA THROUGH YOUR COMPUTER

Until about five years ago, the principal way of obtaining information from the old Lithuanian records was to write to the various Lithuanian archives, asking for details about your family. It was a slow process: when Lithuania regained its independence in 1990 with the dissolution of the USSR, the archives had neither the resources to computerize their records, nor the manpower to deal with the new flood of enquiries from researchers seeking their Jewish roots. All enquiries had to be researched individually, and responded to in writing. There was such a backlog that it usually took a minimum of about nine months before any information came back to a researcher, and this would be restricted to details of the particular family which was the subject of the enquiry. It was not possible to obtain a copy of an entire list for a particular town. But since about 1998-9, the task of obtaining information from the records housed in the Lithuanian archives has been transformed because of the activities of JewishGen Inc., an American-based internet source for researchers of Jewish genealogy; LitvakSIG, a special interest group formed for research into Lithuanian ancestry; and a number of more narrowly focussed District Research Groups operating under its umbrella, coupled with the ease of exchanging information over the internet.

District Research Groups

The basic idea behind the formation of the District Research Groups was that researchers with a common interest in the towns of a particular *uezd* in Lithuania should come together and, instead of each writing to the archives and paying for an individual search, they should pool their resources, contribute to a common fund, and try to acquire from the archives copies of all the lists relating to all the towns in that district.

48

Reg. #	Last Name	Given Name	Relationship to the Head of Household	Father's Name	Mother	Spouse	Age	Other comments
1	PROP	Abel	Head of household	Shimon		Tamare	56	Resides in Skaudvile, 3rd Guild Merchant
1	PROP	Todres	Son	Abel	Tamare	Leah	27	
1	PROP	Eliash	Son	Abel	Tamare		20	
1	PROP	Meyer	Son	Abel	Tamare		10	
1	PROP	Shimel	Grandchild	Todres	Leah		4 1/2	
1	PROP	Wolf Ayzyk	Grandchild	Todres	Leah		3	
1	PROP	Tamare	Wife			Abel son of Shimon	42	
1	PROP	Tauba	Daughter	Abel	Tamare		16	
1	PROP	Sorka	Daughter	Abel	Tamare		4	
1	PROP	Leah	Daughter-in-law			Todres son of Abel	26	
1	PROP	Sora	Grandchild	Todres	Leah		7	
2	PROP	Iosel	Head of household	Abel		Cherne	37	Resides in Skaudvile, a peddler
2	PROP	Chaim	Son	Iosel	Cherne		15	
2	PROP	Itsyk	Son	Iosel	Cherne		19	
2	PROP	Rafel Shimel	Son	Iosel	Cherne		1	
2	PROP	Cherne	Wife			Iosel son of Abel	35	
2	PROP	Bluma	Daughter	Iosel	Cherne		14	
3	FRIDMAN	Tsalel Mendel	Head of household	Meyer	Feyga	Feyga	40	Resides in Skaudvile, a kosher slaughterer
3	FRIDMAN	Ber	Son	Tsalel Mendel	Feyga		13	
3	FRIDMAN	Feyga	Wife		Feyga	Tsalel Mendel son of Me'	39	
3	FRIDMAN	Ente	Daughter	Tsalel Mendel	Feyga		9	
3	FRIDMAN	Frada	Daughter	Tsalel Mendel	Feyga		4	
4	GAYKHEL	Zalkind	Head of household	Srol		Rivka	70	Resides in Skaudvile, a miller
4	GAYKHEL	Iokhel	Son	Zalkind	Rivka	Paya	40	
4	GAYKHEL	Ber	Grandchild	Iokhel	Paya		13	
4	GAYKHEL	Borukh	Grandchild	Iokhel	Paya		9	
4	GAYKHEL	Leyb	Grandchild	Iokhel	Paya		4	
4	GAYKHEL	Rivka	Wife			Zalkind son of Srol	64	
4	GAYKHEL	Paya	Daughter-in-law			Iokhel son of Zalkind	38	
4	GAYKHEL	Sora	Grandchild	Iokhel	Paya		7	
4	GAYKHEL	Dine	Grandchild	Iokhel	Paya		11	
5	MEURE	Shimon	Head of household	Meyer	Dvera	Dvera	33	Resides in Nemaksciai, a tavern owner
5	MEURE	Movsha Leyb	Son	Shimon	Dvera		9	
5	MEURE	Chaim	Nephew	Meyer			13	
5	MEURE	Movsha	Nephew	Abram			13	

An example of the kind of material e-mailed to members of a District Research Group. This is a translation of an extract from the 1847 Family List for Skaudvile, reformatted in a standard form for documents such as revision lists and family lists. It gives details of all the members of the household, and their relationship to the head of the household.

Record #	Surname	Given Name	Age	Other Comments	Day	Month	Year	Archive/Fond/Inventory/File#
52	ABRAMER	Girsh	55		12	April	1892	Kaunas Regional Archives/I-49/1/16683
53	ABRAMER	Gershon	60		12	April	1892	Kaunas Regional Archives/I-49/1/16683
1	ABRAMOVICH	Leyb	66		12	April	1892	Kaunas Regional Archives/I-49/1/16683
9	ABRAMOVICH	Girsh	55		12	April	1892	Kaunas Regional Archives/I-49/1/16683
73	ABRAMOVICH	Abram	49		12	April	1892	Kaunas Regional Archives/I-49/1/16683
101	ABRAMOVICH	Pinkhus	62		12	April	1892	Kaunas Regional Archives/I-49/1/16683
102	ABRAMOVICH	Shaya	65		12	April	1892	Kaunas Regional Archives/I-49/1/16683
103	ABRAMOVICH	Zelman Movsha	38	did not show up; was out of town	12	April	1892	Kaunas Regional Archives/I-49/1/16683
113	BANDEL	Aron	59		12	April	1892	Kaunas Regional Archives/I-49/1/16683
45	BEDER	Leyb	65		12	April	1892	Kaunas Regional Archives/I-49/1/16683
46	BERELIOVICH	Preydel	28		12	April	1892	Kaunas Regional Archives/I-49/1/16683
28	BERMAN	Orel Iosel	27		12	April	1892	Kaunas Regional Archives/I-49/1/16683
93	BINDER	David	62		12	April	1892	Kaunas Regional Archives/I-49/1/16683
83	BLOKH	Abram	45		12	April	1892	Kaunas Regional Archives/I-49/1/16683
110	BLOKH	Ovsey	50		12	April	1892	Kaunas Regional Archives/I-49/1/16683
36	BLUM	Shmuel	66		12	April	1892	Kaunas Regional Archives/I-49/1/16683
25	BRAUDE	Leyb	49		12	April	1892	Kaunas Regional Archives/I-49/1/16683
65	BRIKER	Iosel	47	did not show up; was out of town	12	April	1892	Kaunas Regional Archives/I-49/1/16683
39	DANILOVICH (?)	Aron	59	did not show up; was out of town	12	April	1892	Kaunas Regional Archives/I-49/1/16683
67	EDELSHTEYN	Abram	55		12	April	1892	Kaunas Regional Archives/I-49/1/16683
70	FAKTOR	Gesel	45	did not show up; was out of town	12	April	1892	Kaunas Regional Archives/I-49/1/16683
79	FEYNZINGER	Abram	43		12	April	1892	Kaunas Regional Archives/I-49/1/16683
107	FOGEL	Ovsey	43		12	April	1892	Kaunas Regional Archives/I-49/1/16683
49	GAK	Ovsey	52		12	April	1892	Kaunas Regional Archives/I-49/1/16683
109	GAUKHMAN	Velvel	52		12	April	1892	Kaunas Regional Archives/I-49/1/16683

Another example of the kind of material e-mailed to members of a District Research Group. This is a translation of an extract from the 1892 Rabbi's Electors List for Silale, re-formatted in a standard form for this type of record. It lists only the heads of the households and their ages.

The scheme has been very successful. There are today 12 District Research Groups in existence, which over the past six or seven years have been purchasing copies of entire lists, having them translated, and inputting the translated material into searchable databases. The lists acquired by them include revision lists, family lists, box and candle tax lists, rabbis electors lists, lists of persons evading military service, and so on. A typical database for a single district may contain as many as 40,000 entries, covering the persons who lived in the 20 or so *shtetlach* in the district over the period from 1816 to about 1914.

As and when a list is acquired and translated, the resultant database is distributed by e-mail to those members of the group who have contributed a minimum of $100 towards its funds. The information is normally sent in Excel spreadsheet format, and once downloaded onto your computer, the material can be sorted in any way that best suits your needs: by surname, by date order, or by town. New members joining a group and contributing a minimum of $100 are sent all the material accumulated to date. Because of the size of the lists, they are generally "zipped" (compressed with Winzip or a similar piece of software). The full lists are normally made available to contributors about a month after they have sent in their contributions, a much faster service than is available through a direct enquiry to the archives. (See the illustrations on pages 49 and 50).

There are also obvious advantages in being able to see a full list of names of all the people recorded for the *shtetl*, as compared to writing to the archives and receiving only an extract from the records about the members of your own family, and to see all the lists, of all kinds, relating to one town, all in chronological order. It is also often helpful to see lists for neighbouring towns, which may help to trace wider family relationships; our ancestors moved around quite freely within the Pale, and members of a family frequently moved on marriage, or to study or work in another *shtetl*.

As at the time of writing, District Research Groups have been established for the following *uezds*:

      Kovno *guberniya*:   Kaunas, Panevezys, Raseiniai, Siauliai, Telsiai and Zarasai

Vilna *guberniya*: Dizna, Lida, Oshmiany, Trakai, Ukmerge and Vilnius.

Suwalki *guberniya*: A research group for the whole *guberniya* does the same collection of material as the District Research Groups.

A current list of the various district research groups, with instructions as to how to contact the group co-ordinators, is available at www.jewishgen.org/Litvak/research.htm.

All Lithuania Database (ALDB)

As the amount of material being collected by the District Research Groups grew, a new idea was born, and that was to construct a single, large, all-embracing searchable database, accessible online and free of charge. Accordingly in 2001 LitvakSIG launched the All Lithuania Database (ALDB), a mega-database incorporating data from many different sources, and which today contains the largest number of Lithuanian Jewish records on the Internet. All the various SIGs have contributed the material collected by them to the ALDB, with the result that it contains data extracted from revision, family and census lists, and district merchants, craftsmen's guilds, farmers, and town residents lists, as well as box tax and candle tax lists, voters lists, etc, from 1765 until the early 20th century, for most of the districts in the old Vilna and Kovno *gubernii*. It has also incorporated information from vital records, and from non-archival sources, such as cemetery lists, the HaMelitz and HaMagid donor lists, and the JewishGen Family Finder. The database is to be found on-line at www.jewishgen.org/Litvak/all.htm and is clearly a very useful tool to help researchers identify the records in which their ancestors are named. Other towns where families with the same name lived can be identified, and researchers may be able to find relations in neighbouring *shtetlach*.

The ALDB can be searched either by town or by surname, and by either the actual name or a soundex equivalent. (See page 60). It has a powerful search engine, and the initial results come up very quickly,

Portion of the first page obtained in an ALDB search for the surname Grin

listing the various types of record in which the town or surname is featured, and the number of entries for each type of record. You can then select the type of record and all the relevant entries will be presented for you to scroll through.

This is an on-going project, and continues to grow as further records are acquired by the various LitvakSIG Research Groups. You should therefore re-visit it from time to time to check whether any new information has been added.

Town Uyezd Guberniya	Surname	Given Name	Father	Relationship	Age This / Age Last	Reason Left / Year	Comments	Date	Page Registration / Former Registration	Publication Type / Archive / Fond etc
Baisogala Siauliai Kaunas	GRIN	Gesel	Yankel	Head of Household	38 / 30			26 May 1858	440 / 32	Revision List LVIA/1262/1/99
	GRIN	Girsha	Gesel	Son	15 / Missing	Expelled / 1875	Converted, Moved to Moscow		25	
	GRIN	Pese	Abram	Wife	?					
	GRIN	Makhle	Gesel	Daughter	?					
	GRIN	Ettel	Gesel	Daughter	?					
Baisogala Siauliai Kaunas	GRIN	Yankel Fayvush	Geshel / Genekh (?)	Head of Household	20			14 October 1866	174 / 32	Additional Revision List LVIA/1262/1/124
	GRIN	Beile		Wife	20					
Seduva Siauliai Kaunas	GRIN	Girsh	Tankhel	Head of Household	40			30 May 1858	530 / 1	Additional Revision List LVIA/1262/1/99
	GRIN	Tankhel	Girsh	Son	15 /	Converted / 1875/74	Moved to Perm. Guberniya			

Stage 2 of the ALDB search: results after clicking on the All Lithuania Revisions List database link

1895-7 All-Russian Census (See page 24 above)
www.jewishgen.org/databases/Lithuania/LithCensus1897.htm

This is a stand-alone database, although its material is incorporated into the ALDB. It can be searched by either surname or town name. It contains the names of 13,465 Jewish individuals (2,475 families) who were residing in Kovno and Vilna *gubernii*.

1816 Revision Lists (See pages 26 and 43 above)

The Jewish Family History Foundation has published a number of the 1816 Revision Lists on its website www.jewishfamilyhistory.org and offers Excel spreadsheets copies for a fee to those who want to work on the lists. As at the date of writing, those published are for the following towns:

> Batakiai, Cekiske, Dotnuva, Dauglaukis (Davkinlava), Erzvilkas, Gaure, Girkalnis, Grinkiskis, Josvainiai, Jurbarkas, Kvedarna, Labunava 1811, Labunava 1816, Nemaksciai, Nemaksciai-Siline, Pajuris, Raseiniai, Ritavas, Seredzius, Silale, Sveksna, Taurage, Upyna, Vainutas, Veliuona, Vidukle, Veivirzenai, Vilkija, and Zemaiciu Naumiestis.

It has also indicated that as and when each *kahal* list of the Grand Duchy of Lithuania censuses of 1765 and 1784 is funded and transliterated, it will publish these on its website.

Lithuania Internal Passports Database   (See page 35 above)

Howard Margol has started to establish a database for the 16,000 Jewish applications for passports in Panevezys, covering the period of 1919-1940. Even though the applicants were living in Panevezys at the time, many of them were born elsewhere in Lithuania, as well as in various parts of Russia. The database containing the first information from the files is now available online at www.jewishgen.org/databases/Lithuania/InternalPassports.htm.

Information provided by the database includes the names of the applicant and members of his family, their residential address, dates of birth, sometimes their place of birth, and a reference to the archive fond where the passport application can be found.

Dedicated *shtetl and uezd* websites

More than 60 websites relating to individual shtetlach have been set up under the JewishGen Shtetlinks programme. They vary in content and style, but many are helpful in tracing relatives. A full list of these can be found on the Shtetlinks website, which is at http://shtetlinks.jewishgen.org/Lithuania.html. (See the illustration overleaf). There is also a dedicated website for the Suvalki *guberniya*: www.jewishgen.org/SuwalkLomza.

JewishGen®
ShtetLinks
preserving our history for future generations

Lithuania

Regional Special Interest Groups:
Litvak SIG | Suwalk-Lomza SIG

- Alytus (Olita)
- **Anyksciai (Anykst)**
  (In Progress. Contact Mindie Kaplan)
- Birzai (Birzh)
- Butrimonys (Butrimoniai) 54°30' / 24°15'
- **Ciobiskis (Czabiski)**
  (In Progress. Contact H. Jay Siskin)
- Dieveniskes (Divinishuk)
- Gargzdai (Gorzd)
- Jonava (Yaneve)
- **Joniskis (Yanishok) 56°14' / 23°37'**
  (In Progress. Contact Rich Lowenthal)
- Joniskelis (Yonishkel)
- Jurbarkas (Yurburg)
- Kaisiadorys (Koshedar)
- Kalvarija
- Kapciamiestis (Kopcheve)
- Kaunas (Kovno)
- Kelme (Kelem)
- Klaipeda (Memel)
- Krakes (Krok)
- Kretinga
- Kupiskis (Kupishok)
- Kudirkos Naumiestis (Naishtot)
- **Kuliai** *(In Progress. Contact Autimas)*
- **Kurkliai** *(In Progress. Contact Dora Boom)*
- **Kvedarna (Chweidan)**
- **Kybartai (Kibart)**
- **Lazdijai (Lazdei)**
- **Luoke** *(In Progress. Contact Joel Fetter)*
- **Lygumai**
- **Maletai (Malat)**
  (In Progress. Contact Joe Winston)
- Marijampole (Mariampol)
- Merkine (Meretch)
- **Moletai (Malat)**
  (In Progress. Contact Joel Ratner)

- Plunge (Plungiany)
- Prienai (Pren)
- Ritavas (Ritove)
- Rumsiskes (Rumshishok)
- Rokiskis (Rokishok)
- Rozalimas (Rozalija)
- Sakiai (Shaki)
- Salantai (Salant)
- Seirijai (Serey)
- Siaulenai (Shavlan)
  (In Progress. Contact Eunice Blecker)
- Siauliai (Shavel)
- **Silale (Shillel)**
  (In Progress. Contact Lorraine Millings)
- Simnas (Simno)
- Skapiskis (Skopishok)
- Skaudvile (Shkudvil)
- Stakliskes (Stoklishok)
- Sudargas (Sudarg)
- Svencionys (Shvintzion)
- Taurage (Tavrig)
- Tauragnai (Toriguin)
- Telsiai (Telz)
- Troskunai (Troshkun)
- Ukmerge (Vilkomir)
- Utyan (Utena)
- Uzpaliai (Ushpol)
- **Vainute** *(In Progress. Contact Martin Isaacson)*
- Varena (Aran)
- Veisiejai (Vishey)
- Vilkaviskis (Vilkovishk)
- Vilnius (Vilna)
- Virbalis (Virbaln)
- Vistytus (Vishtinetz)
- Zeimelis (Zeimys)
- Zelva (Pazelva)
- Zemaiciu Naumiestis (Neishtot-Tavrig)

The ShtetLinks website has a list of sites dedicated to individual shtetlach, with links to these.

The **Kelme Database** www.jewishgen.org/databases/kelme.htm is an index of over 2,000 data records from various sources for the *shtetl* of Kelme, ranging from 1816 to 1944.

SPECIFIC CEMETERIES IN LITHUANIA

*Inscription on memorial stone: "The old Jewish cemetery
Holy is the memory of the dead"*

- **Ariogola Cemetery Database**
  www.jewishfamilyhistory.org/Ariogala%20Cemetery.htm

- **Kaisadorys and Zasliai**
  www.jewishgen.org/litvak/feigmanis.htm

- **Keidan Cemeteries Database**
  . www.jewishgen.org/databases/keidan.htm
  A comprehensive database compiled by Ada Green of names
  and other inscriptions from the tombstones in seven
  Keidaner cemeteries in Keidan itself and also New York and
  Chicago.

- **Kelme Cemetery database**
  www.jewishfamilyhistory.org/Kelme%20Cemetery.htm

- **Kovno Cemetery List**
  www.jewishgen.org/databases/kovnocem.htm   This is a list
  of those who died in the Kovno Ghetto between 18 August
  1941 and 31 December 1943, and were buried there. It is
  considered to be a list of those who died "natural" deaths -

as opposed to those who were murdered by the "killing squads". It contains nearly 900 surnames. The list was produced by the "Chevra Kadisha," the burial society of Viliampole (Viliampoliai, Slabodke, Slobodka). and is held in the archives of the Beit Lochamai HaGetaot (the Ghetto Fighter's Museum) in Israel.

- **Leckava**
  www.jewishgen.org/litvak/leckava.htm

- **Telsiai**
  www.jewishgen.org/litvak/TelsiaiJewishCemetery.htm

- **Vievis**
  www.jewishgen.org/litvak/vieviscem.htm

- **Zeimelis**
  www.jewishgen.org/litvak/Zeimelis.html

- **Zemaiciu Naumiestis**
  www.jewishgen.org/litvak/neistatcem.htm

This building was formerly the synagogue in Seda. Few of the local community records kept in the old synagogues in Lithuania have survived. (See page 39)

58

7

NAMES APPEARING IN THE OLD RECORDS

There are a few things you will need to know when looking up names in the old records.

Transliteration

The first thing to remember is that most of the original records were kept in the Russian language, written in Cyrillic script. The names that you will find in the on-line databases will have been transliterated into Latin characters, and translated into English. There is no standard way of doing this. Do not therefore expect always to find names appearing as they are spelt today, or as you would spell them.

A common example concerns the sound represented in English by the letter H. There is an equivalent sound in Yiddish and in Hebrew, but no exact equivalent sound in Russian. The Russian sound most closely resembling it is represented in English by the letter G. The result is that a name such as Hurwitz may have been recorded as Gurwitz in the original Russian list, and the initial G may have survived as such when the list was transliterated into Latin characters. Similarly Cohen may have been recorded as Kagan, and the common first name Hirsh as Girsh.

Another example concerns the guttural sound represented in Hebrew by the letter *Chet*. There is no single letter used in English to denote this sound. In the Scottish word *Loch* it is represented by the two letters *ch*. Different translators working from a Russian list of names may render it in other ways. So, for example, Bloch may be rendered as Blokh or Block (cf. the illustrations on pages 49 and 50)

Always be aware of the possibility of variant spellings.

- The common ending *–witz*, as in Abramowitz or Jacobowitz, may be rendered in a translated list as *–vitz*, or *-wich*, or *-vich* or *-wicz*.
- Vowel sounds may be rendered differently, eg, Leiser may be rendered as Leyser; Cohen as Kahn; Rosensweig as Rozentzyayg; Meyerowitz as Meirovich or Meerovitz; Friedman as Fridman.
- S and Z are sometimes interchanged.   Sacks may be rendered as Zaks, Shapiro as Zapira; Israel as Izrael.
- J and Y are sometimes interchanged.   Judel may be rendered as Yudel.

The Daitch-Mokotoff Soundex system

Because of the many ways in which a name can be transliterated or spelt, most JewishGen databases allow a search to be made by either an exact spelling, or by what is known as the Daitch-Mokotoff Soundex system. "Soundexing" involves indexing by sound instead of by alphabet: the Daitch-Mokotoff system uses a coding system devised particularly for Jewish surnames to group similar sounds. If you use this system and search, say, for, Katz, the search-engine will at the same time as searching for Katz, search the database for names such as Ketz, Kutz, Kez, Gets, Gats, Gots, Guz, Kirzner, and so on.

Ashkenazi naming patterns

As you acquire more details of your Lithuanian ancestors, you will probably notice that certain first names tend to re-appear in different generations of a particular family. This is because of the Ashkenazi practice of naming a child after a deceased grandparent. This had the result that if there were two siblings who both had sons born shortly after their grandfather died, the two cousins might well have been given the same first name.

This can be a help in establishing family links when going through the old records. If you are working on a list and find, say, a Hirsh ben Jossel and Hirsh ben Reuven with the same surname, and born about the same time, they may well be cousins, with a common grandfather named Hirsh. This is an indication that if you later find a

Hirsh (or Girsh) with that surname in an earlier list, even if you do not find a mention of his children Jossel and Reuven in the same list, he may well be the common grandfather. You will need to examine their ages to see if these are compatible with such a relationship.

See the article *Using Litvak naming patterns to derive names of unknown ancestors* in Avotaynu, Vol XI/3 (1995) at page 22.

Diminutive forms or nicknames

Names appearing in the more informal communal lists (box lists, candle tax lists, etc) often give the person's first name in the form by which he was known in the community (cf. the illustration at page 50). This would usually be a diminutive form or nickname. Here are some of the most common, with their more formal equivalents.

Abba	Abel	Orel	Aharon
Aizik	Yitzchak	Orko	Aharon
Berko	Ber	Ovsey	Yehoshua
Chemiash	Nechanyahu	Shimel	Shimon
Eliash	Eliyahu	Shimko	Shimon
Elko	Eliyahu	Shimsel	Shimshon
Haushel	Yehoshua	Shmerel	Shmeryahu
Itzke	Yitzchak	Shmerko	Shmeryahu
Kivel	Akiva	Shmuylo	Shmuel
Leyzer	Eliezer	Velvel	Wolf
Mordchel	Mordechai	Yankel	Yaakov
Mordko	Mordechai	Yossel	Yosef
Moshko	Moshe	Yudel	Yehuda
Movsha	Moshe		

Yiddish - Hebrew equivalents (Animal names)

Ber	Dov	(Bear)	Leyb	Arye	(Lion)
Hirsh	Tzvi	(Stag)	Wolf	Ze'ev	(Wolf)

If you combine nicknames with Yiddish-Hebrew equivalents, you get more variants. Thus Velvel may be the same name as both Wolf or Ze'ev, and Berko may be the same as both Ber and Dov.

8

OBTAINING INFORMATION FROM THE ARCHIVES IN LITHUANIA

You may wish to contact the Lithuanian archives directly, either because you do not have access to the Internet and the databases available thereon, or because you want something that is not available on the Internet.

There are a number of archives in Lithuania. Each contains entirely different records, no duplication is involved, and they operate independently. One is not a branch of the other. So you will need to identify the appropriate archive that can answer your needs.

Broadly speaking,

- if your *shtetl* was in Vilna *guberniya*, you will need to write to the Lithuanian State Historical Archives in Vilnius (LVIA) for all your needs;
- if your *shtetl* was in Kovno *guberniya*, you will need to write to the LVIA if you want to search a Revision List, but to the Kaunas Regional Archives if you want to search a Family List, or other lists such as Box Tax Lists, Candle Tax Lists, Voters Lists, Property Owners Lists, and so on;
- if your *shtetl* was in Suvalki *guberniya*, you will need to write to the Polish State Archives in Warsaw (AGAD) for 19th century voters lists, and to the LVIA for other types of documents. Also contact the State Archives in Suwalki.

For more precise information as to which archive to write to, visit the Routes to Roots website at www.rtrfoundation.org. It carries a searchable database of all records available in the various Lithuanian and other Eastern European archives for each town. (See the illustration on page 45).

When you write to any of the archives with an enquiry about your family, send the family names (as close as possible to their original Yiddish or Hebrew names, not the Anglicized version), approximate dates, and the name of the town you are researching. Give them the current Lithuanian name of the town, if you can, as there are some towns which share the same or similar Yiddish name.

Although you do not need to send a family tree, a family tree (maximum three generations) can be helpful. Include only those ancestors who were born, married, lived or died in Lithuania.

The LVIA and the Kaunas Archive will send you photocopies of the original records, if requested. The other archives send an abstract of the record. If you are merely making a preliminary enquiry, it is not absolutely necessary to send the research fee with your request. If you know where your ancestors lived, you will be notified as to what records exist for that town, what the research possibilities are, and an explanation of the payment that is required. You can then advise them as to which records you would like copies or abstracts of.

A search of the records for a large city like Vilnius or Kaunas should be done in stages. A 10-year time frame is usually searched. Too many books of records exist for those cities for a more inclusive search to be done.

Your personal check will be acceptable as long as it is drawn on funds that are accepted worldwide and considered as "hard currency" in Lithuania. US Postal money orders are not acceptable overseas.

A)   Lithuanian State Historical Archives (LVIA)

Lithuanian State Historical Archives
Gerosios Vilties 10
Vilnius LT-03134, Lithuania
Tel: (370) (5) 213-74-82; Fax: (370) (5) 213-76-12
e-mail: istorijos.archyvas@centras.lt

This archive contains most of the available Revision Lists and the vital records for the city of Vilnius for the period 1837–1915. As of February 2002 all pre-1940 Jewish records previously stored in Archive (C) were transferred to this archive. Some of these transferred records date back to 1881.

At the time of writing, the LVIA does not as a rule respond to research requests sent by e-mail. The fax machine is also not always in operation. It is therefore advisable to send your request by ordinary mail, and to ask if you may use e-mail in future communications.

Research fees: The Lithuanian Lita is now pegged to the Euro, which makes it easier than it previously was to arrange payment.

A search per surname per town will cost LT 400 - EU 115
Copy of each record: LT 20 - EU 5.79
Translation of each record: LT 52- EU 15
Copy and translation: LT 72 - EU 20

You can write in English. Their response will be in English. Send the names of your family and ancestral town accompanied by EU 115 in the form of a check or money order. There will be an acknowledgement of your request by letter giving you information about your search and indication of the wait period. This can be as long as a year, and sometimes even longer.

B) Kaunas Regional Archives

Kauno Apskrities Archyvas
Maironio g. 28a
LT- 44249 Kaunas Lithuania
Tel: (370) (27) 732-3073
e-mail: archyvas@turbodsl.lt

This archive contains the records of the various administrative bodies in the former Kaunas *guberniya*. The *guberniya* was established only in 1843, so the records do not go back beyond that date. The archive has no original revision lists, but it has some family lists and many box and candle tax lists, and many other types of records for the seven *uezds* of the former Kovno *guberniya*: Kovno, Rosseiny, Telsiai, Siauliai, Ponevezh, Vilkomir (now Ukmerge), and Novo-Aleks-androvsk (now Zarasai).

Research and record fees are the same as for the LVIA. You can write in English. Their response will be in English.

C) Lithuanian Central Civil Register Archives

> Lietuvos Centrinis Metriku Archyvas
> (Lithuanian Central Civil Register Archives)
> Kalinausko 21, 2600
> Vilnius, Lithuania

This archive contains post-1940 vital records.

Research fees: none required. If you want an abstract, the cost will be a maximum of $15 for each record located. You can write in English, but their response will be in Lithuanian.

D) Panevezys Archives

> Panevizio Apskrities Archyvas
> M. Valancianus 3
> Panevezys LT-5319, Lithuania
> Tel/Fax: (370) (45) 46-15-37
> e-mail: archyvas@post.omnitel.net

This archive contains post-World War II records, including a small number of Jewish records: 1940 Panevezys Jewish property records, a 1947 request of the Panevezys Jews for the return of a synagogue, etc.

Research and record fees are the same as for the LVIA. Write to them in Lithuanian or Russian. They are unable to translate English.

E) Panevezys Civil Register Archive

> Panevezio Skyrius Civilines Metrikacijos Archyvas
> Respublikos 25
> Panevezys, Lithuania

This archive contains post-1940 vital records. Write to them in Lithuanian or Russian. They are unable to translate English. Research and record fees are the same as for the LVIA.

F) Lithuanian Archive of Image & Sound

This archive is part of the Central State Archives:

> **Lithuanian Central State Archive (LCVA)**
> O. Milasiaus 21
> Vilnius 10102, Lithuania
> Tel: (370) (52) 47-78-29
> e-mail: lvga@takas.lt and lcva@takas.lt

This archive contains the photographs of 1222 Jewish Russian Army conscripts, 1900-1914, from the Vilnius District. www.jewishgen.org/databases/VilnaConscriptsPhotos.htm and www.mindspring.com/~peggyf/Lithuania/jewish-conscripts.htm

The archive also contains numerous photographs of Jewish subjects in Lithuania that were taken during the 1920-1930s. www.mindspring.com/~peggyf/Lithuania/ais.htm

Other archives

Some of the old Lithuanian records are stored elsewhere than in the Lithuanian Archives. Voter registration lists are in Moscow, as are the bulk of military records. Some police records are located in Moscow and in St. Petersburg. A sizeable quantity of the Lithuanian records for the southwestern area of present day Lithuania are stored in the Suwalki archive, and in the Polish State Archives (AGAD) in

Warsaw. See generally www.jewishgen.org/infofiles/polandv.html and the Route to Roots site at www.rtrfoundation.org.

State Archive in Suwalki
ul. Kosciuszki 69
Suwalki 16-400, Poland
Tel: (48) (87) 565-0185

Polish State Archives-AGAD
(Central Archives of Historical Records)
ul. Dluga 6, skr. poczt. 1005
Warszawa 00-950, Poland
Tel: (48) (22) 831-5491
e-mail: archagad@poczta.onet.pl

The town of Klapeida, on the Baltic coast, is now part of Lithuania but was previously part of East Prussia, and was known as Memel. The **Memel Archives** had a collection of pre-World War 1 records, written mainly in German. These records are now dispersed, with about one-third in the Central State Archives in Vilnius, (see under F above) and one-third in an archive in Berlin. For more information see www.judeninostpreussen.de or contact the Lithuanian Central State Archives (F above).

Personal visits to the archives

To a limited extent it is possible for you to go to Lithuania and do your own research. But note that you will need to be able to read and translate Russian Cyrillic writing. Pre-World War I records are in Russian Cyrillic. Jewish vital records are in Cyrillic and duplicated in Hebrew or Yiddish. Post-World War I records are in Lithuanian. You would also have to spend several weeks in the archives in order to get any results. The archivists do not encourage individuals to do their own research due to the fragile nature of the original records. It is far better to contact the archive or hire a private researcher in Lithuania.

If you do decide to visit the archive personally, you will be well-advised to write to them several months in advance, give them full information as to what you will be looking for, and include the date on which you expect to be at the archive; they will make every effort to have records waiting for you.

Inside the Kaunas Regional Archives

9

LOOKING FOR LEADS IN NON-LITHUANIAN SOURCES

This is primarily a guide to the Lithuanian archival records which you will need to consult when trying to trace ancestors who actually lived in Lithuania. However, you may initially need to consult sources in your own country and elsewhere outside Lithuania in order to obtain some material to start you off on your researches, such as information to identify your ancestral *shtetl*, or your grandfather's Hebrew name, or details of your more immediate ancestors who left Lithuania to settle in the country where you now live. This chapter tells you of the sources where you might find such leads. It is not intended as a complete list of genealogical sources available outside Lithuania, nor as a guide to sources which might help you in finding relatives alive today who are descendants of your Lithuanian forebears.

CEMETERY AND BURIAL RECORDS, OBITUARY NOTICES

Inscriptions on headstones and burial records generally carry the Hebrew name of the deceased's father, and can also be useful in providing dates of birth. Check where your immigrant ancestor is buried. If you do not know the burial site, but know the *shtetl* from which he came, you may find a reference in congregational or *landsmanshaft* plots. Many immigrants belonged to *"landsmanshaftn"*, organizations of people from the same ancestral town, and many of these *landsmanschaftn* had special burial areas set aside for their members in some cemeteries. Synagogues were often comprised of members from the same area of origin. Obituary notices published in local secular and Jewish newspapers often contain more accurate details than official death certificates.

There are two major on-line projects to collect data about Jewish burials and cemeteries. Their websites have very similar URLs, but the two sites are linked. One is the **International Jewish Cemetery Project** initiated by the International Association of Jewish Genealogical Societies (www.jewishgen.org/cemetery). Its mission is to catalogue every Jewish *burial site* throughout the world. It has a listing of over 27,000 cemeteries. The other is the **JewishGen Online Worldwide Burial Registry** (JOWBR), a project to establish a searchable database *of names and other identifying information* from Jewish cemeteries and burial records worldwide, from the earliest records to the present. It is a compilation of two databases: a database of burial records, linked to a database of information about each particular cemetery. It currently contains about 400,000 names. This website is at www.jewishgen.org/databases/Cemetery.

Cemeteries in particular cities (outside Lithuania)

There are a number of dedicated databases for cemetery records of individual cities outside Lithuania, or particular *landsmanshaftn*. The information on most of them has been included in the JOWBR, but some of them have been separately published on the Internet.

Jewish Burial Society plots in the New York Metropolitan Area

The Jewish Genealogical Society, Inc. (New York) has identified the names and cemetery locations of Jewish burial society plots in the New York metropolitan area. These include plots of *landsmanshaftn*. Details are included on a database containing over 10,000 entries from almost 100 cemeteries located in New York City, Long Island, Putnam County, Westchester County and northern New Jersey. You can search for burial plots set aside for your ancestral town on the website at www.jgsny.org/searchcity.htm.

Boston   www.jewishgen.org/databases/advocate.htm
This database is an index of 23,741 obituary notices which appeared in the Boston *Jewish Advocate* from 1905 to January 2004.

Cleveland   www.jewishgen.org/databases/cleveweb.htm
There is a database of 25,493 obituary notices which appeared in the *Cleveland Jewish News* over the period from October 1964 to July 2004.

CENSUS RETURNS

These records are an obvious source of useful genealogical information, but may vary as to the details they carry.

In the UK

A census of the general population is undertaken every 10 years, but the detailed contents are not made public until 100 years after the census date. The last available census is that of 1901. The censuses returns may be examined at the Family Record Centre at Myddelton Street, London. The 1901 census for England and Wales can be searched online on the official Public Records Office website at www.1901census.nationalarchives.gov.uk.

A "free-to-view" online searchable database of the 19th century UK census returns is provided by FreeCen, a volunteer body associated with Free BMD, on its website at http://freecen.rootsweb.com.

In the USA

Federal censuses are taken at the end of every decade. All censuses up to 1930 are public records, but cannot be searched by name. However if you know the state, county, and town in which your ancestor lived in the census year, you can purchase the microfilm for that town.

Write to
  Census Microfilm Rental Program
  PO Box 30
  Annapolis Junction, MD 20701
  Phone: 301 604 3699

Ancestry.com provides a search engine for all the Federal censuses from 1790-1930 on their website www.ancestry.com. The facility is also available on the related site www.rootsweb.com. There is a fee involved.

NATURALIZATION AND RELATED RECORDS

These records can provide a researcher with information such as the date and place of birth of the applicant, occupation, immigration year, marital status and spouse information, and the names and addresses of witnesses.

In the UK

There are two types of naturalization record available at the Public Record Office ("PRO") at Kew:

> • the actual certificate (file reference: HO 334), which will give the name, address, date and place of birth, and the names of parents, spouse and children; and

> • the complete personal file (file reference: HO 144), which may have further documents providing supplementary information

The PRO does not offer a "search by post" service; you need to go to Kew and do your own research. You will need to start by looking up the surname in the index books (file reference: HO 1), which will give you references to the number of the naturalization certificate, and the number of the complete personal file. There is an on-line search facility at www.catalogue.nationalarchives.gov.uk/search.asp. Type in the surname in the first box, and "HO" in the "Department Code" box. See the article in Shemot, Vol.13, No 2 (June 2005).

In the USA

In the USA, most naturalization records are stored at county courts. For information on obtaining access to them, see the website of the National Archives and Records Administration at www.archives.gov/research_room/genealogy/research_topics/natur alizationrecords.html.

The Ancestry website http://landing.ancestry.com/immigration/immigration_records.aspx and its associated site www.rootsweb.com provide details of all naturalizations from 1700 to 1900.

Alien Registration. All non-citizens were required after 1940 to register. To obtain information from these records, write to U.S. Citizenship and Immigration Services (USCIS), Freedom of Information, Room 5304, 425 I Street NW, Washington, DC 20536. (202) 514-1554.

Social Security Applications. Because legal aliens in the U.S. can obtain a Social Security card, their names may appear in the Social Security Death Index if their deaths were reported. Records of these applications go back as far as 1937. The application form asks for "Birthplace" - often the town name was filled in. You will need to know the social security number of the person concerned. To find this, you can use the Ancestry Social Security Death Index www.ancestry.com/ssdi. This is an index to US residents with Social Security numbers whose deaths were reported to the Social Security Administration (SSA). The SSA used a computer database from 1962 for processing requests for benefits.

In South Africa

A register compiled in 1907 by the Cape Jewish Board of Deputies of Jewish applications for naturalization made during the years 1903-1907 in what was then the Cape Colony is stored in the archives of the Isaac and Jessie Kaplan Centre for Hebrew and Jewish Studies at the University of Cape Town. This register was made as part of a report requested by the Colonial Secretary at the time, and is not necessarily a complete list of all Jewish applications: there are only 1,253 entries. Professor Aubrey Newman of Leicester University has computerized the 1,253 entries, but they are presently unavailable to the general public. A sample database in Excel spreadsheet format that has approximately 1,000 of the entries has been compiled and sorted into alphabetical order by Ann Rabinowitz, and can be downloaded from a link at www.jewishgen.org/SAfrica/natrec.htm.

The registers represent a small proportion of those who were naturalized during the period of 1903 through 1907. The full range of these records can be found in the Family History Library (see page 80 below) and in the South African Archives, where they are computerized. Search must however be done by the researcher in person.

A general source in South Africa is the National Automated Archival Information Retrieval System (NAAIRS) which is a catalogue of the archival holdings of the National Archives and Provincial Archives Services, and incorporates the national registers of non-public records in a range of other archival repositories. This database does not reflect the actual contents of the archival material, but provides a reference to the material in an archive repository. Having identified relevant material, the user must then make contact with the relevant archive repository to consult the document, quoting the source code, volume number and reference number.

All enquiries regarding genealogical research may be directed to Enquiries@dac.gov.za

PASSENGER AND SHIPPING LISTS

These can be helpful in tracing your *shtetl* as they sometimes give the name of the town in which the passenger lived, although often the place of origin is given simply as "Russia" or "Kovno". (See page 19 above)

In the UK

The Public Record Office at Kew has records of people *leaving* British ports between 1878 and 1888, and between 1890 and 1960 (Reference BT 27), but there are no records in the UK of persons *entering* the UK from elsewhere in Europe. This means that you cannot trace the arrival in the UK of your Lithuanian ancestors through shipping records, but if any family members were in transit to America, South Africa or Australia, you may be able to find a reference to them. The PRO does not offer a "search by post" service; you need to go to Kew and do your own research.

There is a large scale project currently being undertaken by the Isaac and Jessie Kaplan Centre for Hebrew and Jewish Studies at the University of Cape Town to create an online database of all passengers who passed through England on their way to South Africa by ship.

London Poor Jews Temporary Shelter Database
http://chrysalis.its.uct.ac.za/shelter/shelter.htm

In the absence of passenger records, this database may be helpful in providing some limited information. The Poor Jews' Temporary Shelter was established in London, England, in 1885 to serve the needs of Jews who were arriving by ship in London, and passing through to other destinations. The names and various other pieces of information about each new arrival to the Shelter were recorded by hand in a series of Registers covering the period 1896-1914. The information has been recorded in a database, in a project designed by Professor Aubrey Newman and Dr. Graham Smith of the Departments of History and of Computer Science respectively in the University of Leicester. The database was created and is maintained by the Leicester Department of History, but is presented on the Internet by the Isaac and Jessie Kaplan Centre for Hebrew and Jewish Studies at the University of Cape Town.

For more information about the Shelter, including photographs and copies of the annual reports, see
www.movinghere.org.uk/galleries/histories/jewish/journeys/thames 5.htm.

Meirowitz, J	
ID(UCT)	40762
Reg. Volume	6
Ref. Nr.	4401
Date entered.	28-10-1903
First name	J
Surname	Meirowitz
Gender	
Age	38
Birthplace	Russia
Mar. Status	m
Nr. of Children	1
Place from	Libau
Occupation	dealer
In via	
Stay	1
Date left	1903.10.29
Place to	Africa
Eventual dest.	
Ship	Braemar Castle
Agent	
Notes	Came on ship Vicking.

The type of information available from the Shelter database (see page 75)

In the USA

The best-known and most publicized immigration portal in the USA is undoubtedly Ellis Island, in the port of New York, but it was by no means the only one. There were five major ports in the USA through which immigrants entered between 1820 and 1940: New York, Baltmore, Boston, Philadelphia and New Orleans, plus a number of minor ports. Passenger arrival lists exist for all these ports. These contain a column for "Last Residence", which might be town, province, or country, depending upon the ship. Lists after 1906 always contain a "Birthplace" column (city and country), and can be seen online. For a list of where these lists can be found, see the indexes compiled by Joe Beine, at
http://home.att.net/~wee-monster/passengers.html and
http://home.att.net/~wee-monster/passengerlists.html.

The Ellis Island arrival lists are available online on a database. The official site is www.ellisisland.org/search/passSearch.asp?, but JewishGen offers a one-stop search facility devised by Stephen Morse at www.jewishgen.org/databases/EIDB.

A comprehensive database of passenger and immigration records relating to all ports of entry is available from Ancestry.com http://landing.ancestry.com/immigration/immigration_records.aspx.

In South Africa

The Isaac and Jessie Kaplan Centre for Hebrew and Jewish Studies at the University of Cape Town has a collection of passenger arrival registers arranged in three books covering the periods from 1924 to 1929, with entries for approximately 16,000 passengers. They list the name of the steamship, the date of arrival, and the name and other details concerning the passengers, including the places from which they have come. The material is at present available only to on-site researchers. There is no search capability, but the records are being computerized. For further information, go to the JewishGen Southern Africa SIG's website www.jewishgen.org/SAfrica/sa.htm, where they are described as "immigration registers".

Hamburg emigration lists

Many of the emigrants from Eastern Europe passed through the port of Hamburg. Some 80% of these traveled to the United States. Full lists of embarking passengers were kept. These contain details of the place of origin of the passengers, which might sometimes have been a town, at other times a country. In May 1999 the Hamburg State Archives began the digitization of personal information for the five million persons who emigrated from Hamburg between 1850 and 1934, and since then it has progressively made this information available on the Internet. Initially the online database will cover the years 1890 to 1914.

The official website is at http://linktoyourroots.hamburg.de, but there are a number of other websites which offer search facilities. Search in Google under "Hamburg Emigration Lists".

JEWISHGEN DATABASES

JewishGen maintains a number of databases containing data not obtained from Lithuanian records, but submitted by researchers or other compilers, which may provide leads for your research. Where apposite, the contents of these are now also included in the ALDB, but the original databases can still be accessed separately if required:

- the **JewishGen Family Finder** www.jewishgen.org/jgff. This is a compilation of surnames and towns currently being researched by Jewish genealogists worldwide. It contains requests for links on some 90,000 ancestral surnames and 20,000 town names, and is indexed and cross-referenced by both surname and town name (See also page 20, and the illustration at page 47);

- the **Family Tree of the Jewish People** www.jewishgen.org/gedcom is a compilation of data on individual family trees submitted by researchers, and contains nearly three million names;

- the **ShtetlSeeker** enables one to identify and locate all the various *shtetlach* in central and eastern Europe. www.jewishgen.org/ShtetlSeeker

VITAL RECORDS

In the UK

In order to obtain a copy of a birth, marriage or death certificate, a reference must first be found by searching the national birth, marriage and death indexes which are kept at the Family Record Centre at Myddelton Street, London. These are each divided into quarterly volumes, with the names for each quarter listed alphabetically. For fuller information see the JewishGen InfoFile by Joe Ross at www.jewishgen.org/InfoFiles/uk-rec.txt.

A free online searchable index for England and Wales has been undertaken by FreeBMD, a volunteer organization that has already indexed more than 62 million names between the years of 1837 and 1983, and more names continue to be added everyday. It is estimated that more than 50% of the names between 1837 and 1900 have been indexed. http://freebmd.rootsweb.com

In the USA

The **Ancestry** website www.ancestry.com/search/obit, and its related site www.rootsweb.com provide a comprehensive search engine for births, deaths, marriages and obituary notices.

The **Family History Library (FHL)** has the world's largest collection of birth, marriage and death statistics. (See overleaf).

Visit the website of **The National Center for Health Statistics** for addresses of where to write for vital statistics on a state-by-state basis: www.cdc.gov/nchs/howto/w2w/w2welcom.htm

YIZKOR BOOKS

Yizkor books are memorial books published after World War II by survivors of European Jewry to memorialize the towns destroyed in the Holocaust. More than 1,200 have been published, each for an individual town or region. Most are written in Hebrew and Yiddish.

Although they deal mainly with the town for which they are named and its Jewish community as a whole, they may provide information for researchers who want to identify ancestors who once lived in the town. Many contain a necrology - a list of those from the town who died in the Holocaust, and often some mention of whole families who perished, by survivors who recall them. There may also be a list of survivors, with addresses. There are usually personal memoirs of survivors about their individual families, with names, ages and sometimes birth dates. There are frequently photographs of various communal organizations, with names of the persons pictured. For more about Yizkor Books, see the article by Gary Mokotoff at www.avotaynu.com/holocaust/yizkor2.htm

The largest collection is at Yad Vashem in Jerusalem, but there are many large collections all over the world. The New York Public Library has a collection of 700 Yizkor books.

See generally page 87 below in the chapter on Holocaust Research.

OTHER POTENTIAL SOURCES IN THE USA

Family History Library (FHL). This is the library of the Church of the Latter Day Saints (LDS), more commonly known as the Mormons. Located in Salt Lake City, Utah, the FHL is the main repository for most of the genealogical information the Church has collected. It contains a variety of records from all over the world that can help with family history and genealogical research: vital records; census returns; court, property, and probate records; cemetery records; emigration and immigration lists; printed genealogies; and family and county histories. The FHL's computer system also contains several large databases, some with millions of names. They include the Ancestral File, the Pedigree Resource File, the Vital Records Index, and the International Genealogical Index. You can access these databases on the Internet at www.familysearch.org.

There are more than 3,500 branches of the Library around the world, called Family History Centres. Most of the microfilm and electronic data collections are accessible at these centres. If they are not available at any particular Centre, a copy can be ordered from the FHL. The main UK branch is at Exhibition Road, Hyde Park, London.

The FHL has been active in micro-filming records from various Eastern European archives, and has a large holding of materials of Jewish interest. A comprehensive list of these is available online at www.jewishgen.org/databases/FHLC

Ancestry www.ancestry.com This site claims to have the largest collection of family history records on the web. You can search the US census records, immigration records, passenger records, vital statistics, obituary notices, historical newspapers and city and other directories. A fee is required for some searches. See also its related website www.rootsweb.com

The YIVO Institute for Jewish Research in New York City (15 West 16th Street, New York, NY 10011; Tel 212-246-6080; fax 212-292-1892) has a large Lithuanian collection of materials from the period between the two World Wars entitled "Lithuanian Communities in the Interwar Period" (Record Group 2). This is comprised of original documents the local community administrations received from, and sent to, central government and other communities, and records they maintained to manage the affairs of their local community. (See the article by Deena A Berton at www.jewishgen.org/Litvak/yivo.htm).

World War I Draft Registration Cards, 1917-1918. These were issued to men born between 1886 and 1897 (whether citizens or aliens). They give the exact place of birth: city/town, state/province, country. See FHL under the heading "UNITED STATES - MILITARY RECORDS - WORLD WAR, 1914-1918"; or write to the National Archives Southeast branch.

Probate Records. Wills and records of deceased estates can contain clues. These are filed on the county level. Addresses of all U.S. county courthouses can be found in *Ancestry's Red Book,* or E. P. Bentley's *County Courthouse Book* (Genealogical Publishing Co., 2nd ed., 1995, ISBN 0-8063-1485-0).

JewishGen databases. (USA data) There are a large number of specialized databases (relating, amongst other things, to marriages, marriage announcements, obituaries, and immigrant arrivals) on the

JewishGEN website. Go to www.jewishgen.org/databases and scroll down to "America".

SOUTH AFRICAN SOURCES

A large emigration of Lithuanian Jews to South Africa started in about 1893 when two UK based steamship companies sailing between England and South Africa employed agents in Lithuania to sell passages to South Africa. Very often some members of one family found their way to South Africa, while others moved to the United States, the United Kingdom or Australia. Therefore even if your immediate family settled in the UK or the USA, it is often possible to find records of uncles, cousins or other members of the family who made the move to South Africa.

The JewishGen Southern Africa SIG website www.jewishgen.org/SAfrica/formal sources has information on the following topics, including links to some lists:

- Burials and Cemeteries
- Census Records
- Records of Emigration from Great Britain
- Department of Home Affairs
- Naturalisation Records
- Shipping & Passenger Records
- Sources

The archives of the South African Jewish Board of Deputies in Johannesburg contain a number of *Landsmanschaftn* Records. See the article by Ada Greenblatt on the JewishGen Southern African SIG website at www.jewishgen.org/litvak/salandsrec.htm.

The Central Archives for History of the Jewish People at Beit Hatefutzoth in Jerusalem has a collection of microfilms from the SA Jewish Board of Deputies in Johannesburg, South Africa, which contain information on a number of communal organizations. For a full list see www.jewishgen.org/SAfrica/cahjp-1.htm. Generally on South African sources, and for addresses, see the two JewishGen

82

InfoFiles (Parts A and B) by Saul Issroff at websites www.jewishgen.org/InfoFiles/za-infoa.txt and www.jewishgen.org/InfoFiles/za-infob.txt.

ISRAELI SOURCES

The most important source in Israel is **Yad Vashem**. They will provide names of victims from each shtetl, Pages of Testimony relating to the destruction of the community, eye-witness accounts and memoirs. Their web-site is at www.yad-vashem.org.il (See page 88 below).

> POB 3477
> Jerusalem 91034
> Phone: 972-2-6443400
> Fax: 972-2-6443443
> E-mail: Names.research@yadvashem.org.il

The **Israel Genealogical Society** http://www.isragen.org.il has six branches: Jerusalem, Tel-Aviv, Netanya, the Negev, Haifa/Northern Israel and Beit Shemesh. It has a full range of activities at each of its branches and its members run a variety of Special Interest Groups (SIGs). It offers its services in finding Israelis who have submitted Pages of Testimony to Yad Vashem, or details of the victims. Go to its website and look under "Projects" on the side bar, where you will see a category called "Searching for Submitters of Pages of Testimony in Israel".

Beit Hatefutzoth: The Douglas E. Goldman Jewish Genealogy Center at Beit Hatefutzoth was one of the three parties who came together in October 1999 to combine their three databases to form the Family Tree of the Jewish People: (the other two were the International Association of Jewish Genealogical Societies and JewishGen). This valuable resource is available on site at the museum. Visitors can search a computerized database on which almost 2,000,000 names have already been entered.

Beit Lochamei HaGetaot has partisan records and records of Lithuanian Jews in Estonia etc.

There are a number of groups with particular interest in Lithuania. They are:

o **The Association of Lithuanian Jews** (Igud Yotzei Lita)
   David Hamelech 1
   POB 16352
   Tel Aviv
        Web-site: www.lithuanianjews.org.il

o **Special Interest Group for Lithuania.** The Co-ordinator is Rose Lerer Cohen, and her e-mail address is rlc@shani.net

o **Association of Immigrants from Vilna and Surroundings**
   Bet Vilna
   Sderot Yehudit 30
   POB 11293
   67016 Tel Aviv

None of these organizations is equipped to do genealogical research for you.

A full list of archives and libraries in Israel is available on the website of the Israel Genealogcal Society www.isragen.org.il/ROS/ARCHIVES/archive-resources-index.html.

OTHER SOURCES AVAILABLE ON THE INTERNET

HaMelitz Lithuanian and Latvian Donors:
www.jewishgen.org/databases/hamelitz.htm. The names of almost 20,000 Lithuanian and Latvian charity donors for the years 1893 to 1903 are listed in a database, translated and compiled by Jeffrey Maynard from this Hebrew periodical. The Hebrew University of Jerusalem has an online collection of several early Hebrew newspapers including HaMelitz and HaMagid. The following URL will take you to the English language home page http://jnul.huji.ac.il/dl/newspapers/eng.html. Copies of HaMelitz are also available in the New York Public Library.

BROIDA	Dvora			Kelme, Lith.	Hamelitz #123	1897
BROIDA	Moshe father of Sarah			Kelme, Lith.	Hamelitz #112	1898
BROIDA	Sarah bas Moshe wife of Yitzchok Mordechailowitz			Kelme, Lith.	Hamelitz #112	1898
BROIDA	Shmuel			Kelme, Lith.	Hamelitz #56	1899
BROIZ	Etil			Kelme, Lith.	Hamelitz #229	1902
CHASID	Yehuda Leib	deceased		Kelme, Lith.	Hamelitz #240	1894
DRUZINSKI	Chaya bas Moshe wife of Chaim Tzvi Fridman from Girtagole (Girkalnis)	wed in Kelme 14 Elul		Kelme, Lith.	Hamelitz #229	1902
DRUZINSKI	Dina			Kelme, Lith.	Hamelitz #229	1902
DRUZINSKI	Dishe			Kelme, Lith.	Hamelitz #229	1902
DRUZINSKI	Moshe father of Chaya			Kelme, Lith.	Hamelitz #229	1902
EITZIKZON	Pinchos	came from Africa		Kelme, Lith.	Hamelitz #123	1897
FEIN	Eli			Kelme, Lith.	Hamelitz #123	1897
FEIN	Eliahu			Kelme, Lith.	Hamelitz #56	1899
FEIWELZON	Eli Meir	Rabbi from Kelme appointed ABD Kruk		Kelme, Lith.	Hamelitz #123	1897
FINKELSHTEIN	Rivka bas Yedidia wife of Moshe Rabinowitz	wed 2 Shevat		Kelme, Lith.	Hamelitz #56	1899
FRIDLAND	Feie			Kelme, Lith.	Hamelitz #229	1902
FRIDMAN	Ch			Kelme, Lith.	Hamelitz #229	1902
FRIDMAN	Chaim Tzvi			Kelme, Lith.	Hamelitz #56	1899
FRIDMAN	Devorah			Kelme, Lith.	Hamelitz #229	1902
GOLDBERG	Yosef ben Boruch			Kelme, Lith.	Hamelitz #132	1900

Part of the HaMelitz list of charity donors from the town of Kelme 1895-1902

HaMagid Lithuanian Donors :

www.jewishgen.org/databases/hamelitz.htm   The names of 5,000 donors to Persian famine relief in 1871-72 are listed in a database translated and compiled by Jeffrey Maynard from another early Hebrew periodical.

Sugihara Database

www.jewishgen.org/databases/sugihara.htm This database contains the names and visa dates of 2,139 Lithuanian, Polish, German, and Russian Jews, all of whom were saved by passports issued by the Japanese diplomat Chiune Sugihara, who was stationed in Kaunas. At the end of July, 1940 Sugihara and his wife spent four long weeks writing visas by hand. Of the almost 6,000 Jews with Sugihara visas, most ended up in Kobe, Japan until after the war.

Vsia Vilna 1915 Database

www.jewishgen.org/Litvak/VsiaVilna.htm This database by Scott Noar contains over 17,400 entries from the 1915 city directory for Vilnius, Lithuania.

Lithuanian Medical Personnel

www.jewishgen.org/Litvak/medical.htm Information about 874 Jewish medical personnel, found in two Lithuanian medical directories, 1923 and 1925. Compiled by Harold Rhode.

10

HOLOCAUST RESEARCH

INFORMATION ABOUT VICTIMS AND SURVIVORS

It will be readily apparent that there can be no definitive or complete list of all those who perished in the Holocaust, or of where and how they died.   Millions died, often whole families with no survivors to tell what happened.   Records exist, but are not complete.   Many organizations and interest groups have made their own efforts to establish lists of victims and survivors, but no one list claims to be complete.

The **International Tracing Service** in Arolsen, Germany maintains a master index of information relating to more than 14 million individuals. More information is available from their website http://summitcounty.redcross.org/INTL%20Tracing%20Services.htm, or the Service can be contacted directly at:

> International Tracing Service
> Grosse Allee 5-9
> 34444 Arolsen, Germany

The **American Red Cross** runs a Holocaust and War Victims Tracing Center, a national clearing-house for United States residents seeking the fates of relatives missing since the Holocaust and its aftermath. Their website is at www.redcross.org/services/intl/holotrace.

YIZKOR BOOKS

Over a thousand separate memorial books, focusing on a particular town or a region, have been published to document the fate of those who perished. Such books are usually intended to be a memorial to the town community that was destroyed, as well as to the individuals living there who lost their lives in the Holocaust, and so detail the history of the town and its Jewish community. Most are written in Hebrew or Yiddish. (See also at page 79 above).

The JGSGB has a project to publish a list of Yizkor books available in academic and Jewish libraries in Great Britain, prepared by Saul Issroff and Cyril Fox, which should be available during the course of 2005.

The most helpful sources of Holocaust information are the number of databases with details of victims and survivors which are available on the Internet.

The Central Database of Shoah Victims' Names: Yad Vashem

Yad Vashem is attempting to document each individual who died in the Holocaust. They have a huge microfilm collection of names from the International Tracing Service in Arolsen, Germany. They have also collected Pages of Testimony, provided by those with knowledge of the victims. Their efforts have resulted in the most extensive list of Jewish Holocaust victims, but it, too, is incomplete. The list is published on the www.yadvashem.org website.

JewishGen Holocaust database

JewishGen has a website on which it has published an on-line database which incorporates data from a number of different databases containing information about Holocaust victims and survivors. This is an ongoing project, and at the time of writing already incorporates information from 74 different databases. The URL is www.jewishgen.org/databases/Holocaust.

The JewishGen Yizkor Book Necrology database

This is at www.jewishgen.org/databases/yizkor. It indexes the names of persons in the lists of Holocaust martyrs published in the Yizkor Books appearing on the JewishGen Yizkor Book Translation Project. This database is only an index of names; it directs researchers back to the Yizkor Book itself, where fuller information may be available. This database allows the surnames to be searched via soundex. It currently contains over 3,600 entries from the necrologies of the following 10 Lithuanian towns:

> Dieveniskes (241 entries), Gargzdai (27), Jurbarkas (585), Kybartai (152), Marijampole (1,121), Merkine (231), Plunge (42), Rokiskis (165), Švencionys (including Nemencine, 988 entries), and Zelva (73 entries).

The New York Public Library's Digital Yizkor Book Viewer project

The NYPL has a collection of 700 Yizkor books. The contents of hundreds of 650 of these can currently be viewed online at www.nypl.org/research/chss/jws/yizkorbookonline.cfm. The best way to consult the database is to use the search facility on the Stephen Morse portal at http://stevemorse.org.

United States Holocaust Museum in Washington, DC.

The Benjamin and Vladka Meed Registry of Jewish Holocaust Survivors at the Museum has over 185,000 records documenting the lives of survivors and their families. Although most of the survivors who have registered live in North America, the Museum now includes the names of survivors from all backgrounds living all over the world. www.ushmm.org/remembrance/registry.

The **Lithuanian Central State Archives**, O. Milasiaus 21, Vilnius 2016, Lithuania, have some records of Jews killed in the Holocaust.

Vilna Ghetto Lists

The Jewish State Museum of Lithuania, Pamenkalnio 12, 2001, Vilnius, Lithuania has produced lists of the 15,300 Jews who were in the Vilnius ghetto in 1942, including additional information about each one, and the names of all of the Jews who were in various work camps in the area just outside Vilnius The lists are published in two volumes.

11

A CASE STUDY

This is an account of my personal research into the Lithuanian antecedents of my paternal grandfather. As my ancestral *shtet* was in Kaunas *guberniya,* all but one of the Russian revision lists pertaining thereto were lost. This case study is offered as a practical demonstration of how the information and clues provided by other documents in the Lithuanian archives can be used in researching one's ancestry, and how it is possible even with those limited resources to trace one's roots as far back as about 1720.

I started my research in 1997, before the District Research Groups had been established, and before any computerized databases were available. At that time the only way to obtain information from the various archival documents was by writing to the various archives. Today access to information is so much easier, but the manner in which the material is used remains the same.

Received family history

I started my research with very little anecdotal family history. Like most of us, I became interested only after it was too late to ask questions. So I had only the bare facts that:

- my father, Chaim Aaron, was born in 1887, had emigrated to South Africa in 1906, and was followed two years later by an older brother, Shimon;
- they came from a Lithuanian *shtetl* which they used to refer to as Chwodan;
- they left behind them their parents, and a number of siblings. I knew very little about them, save that my grandfather's name was Shmuel and that as I was named after him, he must have died before I was born. I knew that one of my father's siblings was a brother named Zusman;

- my father had a cousin living in South Africa, Boruch Aaron, who had also lived in Chwodan. His father Meyer was my grandfather's brother.

First steps

I began with very little knowledge of how to go about things. I consulted a map of Lithuania, and tried to find Chwodan on it, but there was no such name. The nearest I could get to a similar-sounding name was Keidan. I had seen the address of the Historical Lithuanian Archives in Vilna on the FAQ provided by JewishGen, and so my first step was to write to them asking whether they could give me any information about the family of a Shmuel Aaron who had lived in the *shtetl* Chwodan (possibly Keidan?)

It was about 6 months before I had a reply. I was told that there were indeed records of Aron families who had lived in Keidan, but that my father's *shtetl* was more probably the town now known as Kvedarna. There were records of some Aron families in that town also, and that if I sent the Archives $50, they would send me the details.

A further number of months went by before I received these details. It turned out that no revision lists for Kvedarna had survived, but that there were some entries for Kvedarna on an 1816 Additional Revision List for Raseiniai district. This included details of 5 families named Aron registered in Kvedarna in that year. These were:
- Aizek ben Girsh, born 1775, his wife Chaie and their 3 children
- Shmuel ben Hirsh, born 1780, his wife Tzipa and their 2 children
- Abram-Kussel ben Hirsh, born 1787, his wife Chaie and their 3 children
- Shmuel ben Leibe, born 1763, his wife Genah
- Leibe ben Meyer, aged twenty-something (the record was illegible).

There was no way of knowing whether any of these were related to me, but the fact that two of the persons were named Shmuel gave me some hope: it was a possible link to my grandfather, although some 70 years still separated them. The first three men on the list, all with a father named Hirsh (Girsh can be equated with Hirsh), were possibly brothers. It was also possible that Shmuel ben Hirsh and Shmuel ben Leibe were both named after the same grandfather – which would mean that their fathers, Hirsh and Leibe, were brothers.

Could these have been distant antecedents of mine? It looked quite promising, but tantalizing: there was still a 70-year gap to bridge if a link was going to be made, and there were no revision lists for the intervening period which were going to help.

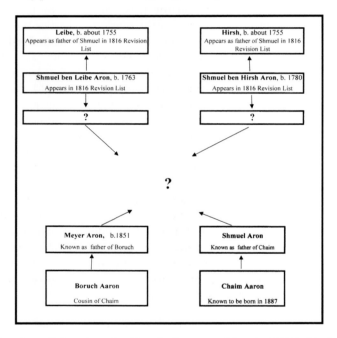

Stage I: Information gathered from family sources and from the 1816 Revision List

The Kaunas archive documents:

I needed first to discover the name of my great-grandfather. My next step was to write to the Kaunas archives to see whether the family name Aron appeared in any other Kvedarna documents.

92

Again it took some time before I received a reply, but in December 1998 the Chief Archivist, Vitalija Gircyte, wrote to say she had managed to find the name in a number of documents pertaining to Kvedarna. She sent me the details, together with typed copies of translations which she herself had made. At first sight the position seemed more confused, rather than clearer. The most comprehensive list of the Jewish community of Kvedarna was a **community list of 1885**. It showed a community of 348 persons, making up 127 different families. There were 16 different Aron households on the list, presumably all descendants of the 5 families shown on the 1816 list, but nothing to indicate how they were linked, and most disappointing of all, no mention of my grandfather Shmuel.

There were however two Shmuel Arons listed on a **List of Real Estate Owners for 1910** (presumably two different persons, one of who might well have been my grandfather), but the document did not give the names of their fathers. I had been hoping to discover the name of my great-grandfather, but this list did not help.

Fortunately, I was able to establish this indirectly. What turned out to be the most useful document was the **list of men from the Raseiniai District who did not report for military duty in 1912**. One of the missing recruits was my father's cousin Boruch, and from the list I was able to obtain details of his father (Meyer), mother and all his siblings. Meyer's father (who was also my grandfather's father) was not named on this list either, but Meyer's age was given as 61 (indicating that he had been born in or about 1851), and this turned out to be significant because it enabled me to link Meyer with an entry on the **1891 list of persons entitled to vote** in the elections for the local administration and the assistant regional rabbi.

On this 1891 list there was a Meyer ben Shimel Aron, aged 40. His date of birth would therefore have been 1851, which was the same as that of the Meyer Aron (Boruch's father) on the military list of 1912. This had to be the same person, which meant that I had now eventually established the name of my great-grandfather: Shimel. If confirmation was needed, it was provided by the fact that Shimel is a common abbreviation for Shimon, and this was consistent with my uncle Shimon (who had emigrated to South Africa) being named after him (his grandfather). (A few years after coming to this conclusion, I was sent a photograph of Meyer's grave, which was in the old Jewish cemetery of Kvedarna. The headstone provided further confirmation that his father's name had been Shimon).

The **1891 voters list** also contained the names of Leib ben Shimel Aron (born 1840) and Girsh ben Shimel Aron (born 1844). These were almost certainly brothers of Meyer: the father's name was the same in all three cases, and their ages were consistent with their being brothers. So I now knew the name of two more siblings of my grandfather. The first names Leib and Girsh had also appeared in the 1816 revision list, so a linkage was becoming more probable.

I could also infer that Shimon Aron, (judging by the age of his oldest son Leib), had probably been born about 1820. He was not mentioned on the 1816 Revision List, so he must have been born shortly after 1816. The gap between the 1816 list and my grandfather was beginning to close.

I now needed to find some mention of Shimon/Shimel himself in an earlier list. Fortunately, there was an **Estimate of Box Tax dated 1850**. This estimate had been drawn up and signed by a number of representatives of the community, and included amongst them was one Shimel ben Zusman Aron. No age was given, but I had earlier inferred that he was probably born about 1817-1820, which would mean he would have been about 30-33 in 1850, when this list was drawn up. This was consistent with his acting as a representative of the community. It seemed I had now determined my great-great-grandfather's identity as Zusman Aron.

This was the first reference to a Zusman Aron that I had come across in the records, but I was mindful of the fact that one of my father's brothers was named Zusman, and this provided some confirmation of a link. Although I had now established the additional fact that Shimon's father had been named Zusman, there was no mention of a Zusman in the 1816 list, so I was still not able to link Shimel Aron, born about 1817-1820, to the families mentioned in the 1816 revision list.

About this time, the District Research Groups were becoming active, and I became a contributor to the Raseiniai District Research Group. The Group Co-ordinator at that stage was David Hoffmann. A year or two later he and his wife Sonia visited Lithuania and obtained access to some of the records of the Grand Duchy of Lithuania censuses in the Vilnius archives. These included the GDL census of the Jewish population of Kvedarna in 1784. These records were in Polish, and the persons listed in it did not yet have surnames. Nevertheless David and Sonia were able to identify two householders named Hyrsz Szmujllowicz and Lejba Szmujllowicz who appeared on this list as the fathers of the Shmuel ben Hirsh Aron and Shmuel ben Leibe Aron mentioned in the 1816 Czarist Revision List. (cf page 31 above).

This meant that, provided that I could link Shimel ben Zusman to either Hyrsz or Lejba Szmujllowicz, I could now take my family tree back another two generations. I could go back as far as their father, Szmujllo, who would have been born about 1720.

David and Sonia had sent me full details of the families of Hyrz and Lejba Szmujllowicz, as they appeared on the 1784 census. These included the names of their children, and I found that the third child of Lejba Szmuilowicz was named Zusman. His age was not given, but if he was aged about 5 or 6, and was born in about 1778, he could quite easily have been the same Zusman who was the father of Shimon, born about 1818.

I was therefore able to conclude that I had probably succeeded in tracing my ancestry, on the paternal side, through Zusman and Lejba, as far back as about 1720-1730.

The tree illustrated overleaf shows what I had been able to learn from the various documents described above. (It shows only the direct line of ascent, although my researches had provided some information about other possible collateral branches).

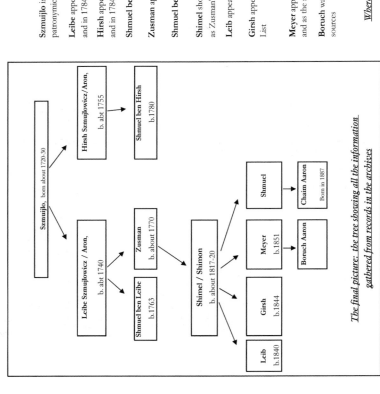

The final picture: the tree showing all the information gathered from records in the archives

Szmujlo is shown as the father of Leibe and Hirsh by their patronymic in 1784 GDL Census

Leibe appears as the father of Shmuel in 1816 Revision List, and in 1784 GDL Census

Hirsh appears as the father of Shmuel in 1816 Revision List, and in 1784 GDL Census

Shmuel ben Leibe appears in 1816 Revision List

Zusman appears as the son of Leiba in 1784 GDL Census

Shmuel ben Hirsh appears in 1816 Revision List

Shimel shown as Meyer's father in 1891 Voters List, and as Zusman's son in 1850 Box Tax Estimate

Leib appears as the son of Shimel in 1891 Voters List

Girsh appears as the son of Shimel in 1891 Voters List

Meyer appears as the father of Boruch in 1912 military list, and as the son of Shimel in 1891 Voters List

Boruch was known to be a cousin of Chaim from family sources

Where the particular items of information came from

96

I have since been able to establish more about some of the other collateral branches descending from Leiba and Hirsh by using another tool available on-line. I had put my name down on the JewishGen Family Finder indicating an interest in the Aaron family from Kvedarna, and through a contact made that way, learnt that one of her descendants living in Kvedarna in the late 19th century had originally borne the surname Aron, but had changed it to Kellman. By carrying out a similar exercise as that described above, I was able to show that this was very probably a branch descended from Hyrsz Szmujilowicz, and to build up a far more detailed family tree.

With the resources that were available to me at the time, the total exercise described above took me some three years. With the facilities now available on-line, it could have been completed in under three months.

The old Jewish cemetery in Kvedarna

12

KEEPING UP-TO-DATE

The resources available to researchers are continually expanding and improving. There are a number of ways in which you can keep yourself up-to-date with the most recent developments.

- Join your local Jewish Genealogical Society. Even if matters specific to Lithuania are not discussed regularly, you can profit by learning of developments of a more general character. Most societies produce a regular magazine with information of new sources. You will also be able to make use of its library facilities.

  The Jewish Genealogical Society of Great Britain has a special interest group for Lithuania that meets two or three times a year.

- Subscribe to an e-mail discussion group. There are a number of these which send members daily e-mails containing requests by other researchers for information, answers to such requests, and up-dates on developments. They provide a regular source of helpful information. No fee is required for joining, and there is no need for subscribers to contribute questions or information, unless they wish to.

  JewishGen runs a discussion group which sends daily bulletins to all subscribers daily via e-mail, as do the LitvakSIG and Shtetlinks, a group of researchers into particular *shtetlach*. Subscribers to these mailing lists share information, ideas, tips, techniques, case studies and resources. Most subscribers are very willing to help others with their queries or difficulties. The electronic mailing list is available in three different modes: Digest, Mail (individual messages), and Index. To join any of these e-mail lists, go to the JewishGen home-page at www.jewishgen.org and scroll down to Discussion Groups.

- There is also a facility to search all past bulletins of these discussion groups. You do not need to be a subscriber to make use of this facility.

- Nor do you need to be a subscriber to read the on-line journal of the LitvakSIG at www.jewishgen.org/Litvak/journal.htm.

- If you have the opportunity, attend one of the annual international conferences on Jewish Genealogy. These meet in a different country every year over a four- or five-day period. The names of the conferences have varied, but since 1998 the name has become standardized as the IAJGS International Conference on Jewish Genalogy. There are normally a number of papers devoted to Lithuanian research, and archivists from the two main Lithuanian archives are usually present to meet with researchers.

- Subscribe to *Avotaynu*, a quarterly journal devoted to Jewish genealogy, published by Gary Mokotoff and Sallyann Amdur Sack, and now in its twentieth year. An on-line index to the main articles that have appeared in the years from 1985-2002 can be found at www.avotaynu.com/subindex/indexl.htm. To subscribe to the journal, go to www.avotaynu.com/journal.htm.

- Gary Mokotoff also edits a monthly e-magazine called *Nu? What's New?* which is e-mailed free of charge to all subscribers. To be added to this mailing list, go to www.avotaynu.com/nuwhatsnew.htm. Back issues of the e-magazine are available at www.avotaynu.com/nu.htm.

SHTETL LOCATOR

There were about 400 *shtetlach* in Lithuania. The location of 150 of these (listed below) is shown on the maps on pages 102-103. Use the grid references in the list to locate your particular *shtetl*.

To find the location of *shtetlach* not on this list, visit the ShtetlSeeker website at www.jewishgen.org/ShtetlSeeker or use www. Mapquest. com.

Akmene	B1	Gargzdai	A1	Kriukai		C1
Alytus	C2	Garliava	C2	Kudirkos	N.	B2
Anyksciai	C1	Gruzdziai	B1	Kuliai		A1
Anteliepta	D1			Kupiskis		C1
Ariogala	B2	**J**iesnas	C2	Kurkliai		C1
		Jonava	C2	Kurkliai		B1
Babtai	C2	Joniskelis	C1	Kursenai		B1
Balbieriskis	B2	Joniskis	B1	Kvedarna		A1
Birstonas	C2	Jubarkas	B2	Kvetkai		C1
Birzai	C1					
Butrimonys	C2	**K**aisiadorys	C2	**L**aukuva		A1
		Kaltaneinai	D1	Lazdijai		B2
Darbenai	A1	Kapciamiestis	B2	Ligumai		B1
Daugai	C2	Kaunas	C2	Linkuva		C1
Dieveniskis	D2	Kavarskas	D1	Lioliai		B1
Dotnuva	C1	Kalvarija	B2	Luksiai		B2
Druskininkai	C2	Kazly Ruda	B2	Luoke		B1
Dukstas	D1	Kedainiai	C2			
Dusetos	D1	Kelme	B1	**M**arijampole		B2
		Krakes	C1	Mazeikiai		B1
Eisiskes	C2	Kraziai	B1	Medninkai		D2
		Krekenava	C1	Merkine		C2
Galvonai	C2	Kretinga	A1	Moletai		D2
Gardai	B1	Kriukai	B2	Mosedis		A1

100

Nemencine	D2	Salcininkai	D2	**U**kmerge	C2
		Salociai	C1	Upina	B1
Obelai	D1	Sartininkai	A2	Upyte	C1
Onuskis	C2	Saukenai	B1	Utena	D1
		Seda	A1	Uzpaliai	D1
Pabaiskas	C2	Seduva	B1		
Paberze	D2	Sesuoliai	C2	**V**abelninkas	C1
Pabile	C2	Seta	C2	Vainutas	A1
Pakruojis	C1	Siaulenai	B1	Valkininkai	C2
Pampenai	C1	Siauliai	B1	Varena	C2
Pandelys	D1	Silale	B1	Varniai	B1
Panemunis	D1	Silule	A1	Veisejai	C2
Panevezys	C1	Siluva	B1	Velvirzenai	A1
Papilys	C1	Simnas	C2	Vidukle	B1
Pasvalys	C1	Sirvintos	D2	Vilnius	D2
Pasvitynis	C1	Skaudvile	B2	Vilvaviskis	B2
Pajuris	A1	Skiemonys	D1	Virbalis	C2
Pilviskiai	B2	Skuodas	A1	Vistytis	C2
Plunge	A1	Stakiai	B2		
Prienai	C2	Stakliskis	C2	**Z**agare	B1
Pusalotus	C1	Subacius	C1	Zapiskis	B2
		Sudargas	B2	Zarasai	D1
Radviliskis	B1	Surviliskis	C1	Zarenai	B1
Raguva	C1	Suwalki	B2	Zeimelis	C1
Ramygala	C1	Svedasai	C1	Zeimelis	D2
Raseiniai	B1	Sveksna	A1	Zelmiai	C2
Rietavas	A1	Svencionaliai	D2	Zelva	C1
Rokiskis	D1	Svencionys	D2	Zemaicius	
Rozalimas	C1			Naumiestis	A1
Rudisikes	C2	**T**aurage	B2		
Rumsiskis	C2	Tauragnai	D1		
		Telsiai	B1		
Sakiai	B2	Trakai	C2		
Salantai	A1	Troskuniai	C1		

101

Baltic Sea

A

B

Skuodas
Mazeikiai
Akmene
Zagare

Mosedis
Saukenai
Joniskis

Seda
Gruzdziai

Salantai
Ligumai

Darbenai
Telsiai
Kursenai

Palanga
Luoke
Siauliai

Kretinga
Plunge
Zarenai

Kuliai

Klaipeda
Gargzdai
Rietavas
Varniai
Gardai
Radviliskis

Velvirzenai
Laukuva
Siaulenai
Kurkliai

1
Kelme
Seduva

Sveksna
Kvedarna
Lioliai

Kraziai
Siluva

Vainutas
Silale
Vidukle

Silute
Pajuris
Raseiniai

Zemaicius Naumiestis
Upina

Taurage
Skaudvile
Ariogala

Sartininkai
Stakiai
Kriukai

Jurbarkas

Sudargas

RUSSIA
Sakiai
Zapiskis

Luksiai

Kudirkos-
Naumiestis
Kazly Ruda

Piliskiai

Vilkaviskis

2
Kybartai
Marijampole

Virbalis
Balbieriskis

Vistytis

Kalvarija

SHTETL LOCATOR

To find the co-ordinates of any
shtetl not on this list, visit
www.jewishgen.org/ShtetlSeeker

For a detailed on-line map of
Lithuania, showing all the towns,
visit www.virtual.lv or
www.mapquest.com

Lazdijai

POLAND

Suwalki

Kapciamiestis

C

D

Kriukai
Zeimelis
Pasvitynis
Salociai
Birzai
Kvetkai
Papilys
Panemunis

Linkuva
Pasvalys
Joniskelis
Pandelys

Vabelninkas
Rokiskis

Pakruojis
Rozalimas
Pampenai
Pusalotus
Kupiskis
Obelai
Dusetos
Uzpaliai
Zarasai

Subacius

Panevezys
Upyte
Krekenava
Raguva
Svedasai
Troskuniai
Anteliepta

Ramygala
Anyksciai
Tauragnai
Dukstas

Krakes
Surviliskis
Kurkliai
Utena
Kavarskas
Skiemonys
Ignalina

Dotnuva
Zelva
Kaltaneinai
Kedainiai

Seta
Ukmerge
Moletai
Zeimiai
Pabile
Pabaiskas
Sesuoliai
Svencionaliai
Svencionys
Zeimilis

Jonava
Babtai
Galvonai
Sirvintos
Paberze

Kaunas
Kaisiadorys
Rumsiskis
Nemencine
Garliava
Jiesnas
Vilnius

Prienai
Trakai
Birstonas
Stakliskis
Simnas
Butrimonys
Rudisikes
Onuskis
Medninkai

Alytus
Valkininkai
Daugai

Varena
Salcininkai
Eisiskes
Dievenis kis

Merkine
Veisiejai
Druskininkai
BELARUS
Lida

1

2

103

APPENDIX A

List of Yiddish and other old shtetl names with current equivalents

Shtetl names have come down to us in various forms: Yiddish, Russian, Polish or German. For genealogical research, it is often necessary to know the current Lithuanian name. This table lists the old forms in alphabetical order, and gives their current equivalents.

There is no accepted "correct" way of rendering Yiddish names into English, and so the spelling of the shtetl names is not always consistent: for example, the Yiddish name for Obeliai may be spelt as either Abel or Obel. It has not been possible to include all possible variants in this table, so if you cannot find a shtetl spelt in the way to which you are accustomed, try other possible variants.

If you are unable to find your shtetl on this list, try the LitvakSig on-line list at www.jewishgen.org/Litvak/Shtetls/Lithuania.htm.

OLD NAME	CURRENT NAME	UEZD	GUBERNIYA
A			
Abel, Abely, Abli	Obeliai	Zarasai	Kaunas
Abolnik	Vabalninkas	Panevezys	Kaunas
Airiogala	Ariogala	Kaunas	Kaunas
Aishishok	Eisiskis	Lida	Vilnius
Akmeyan, Akmian	Akmene	Siauliai	Kaunas
Aleksat. Alexot	Aleksotas	Marijampole	Suwalki
Alite	Alytus	Trakai and Kalvaria	Vilnius and Suwalki
Alshad, Alsiad, Alsian	Alsedziai	Telsiai	Kaunas
Alunta, Avanta, Owanta	Alante	Ukmerge	Kaunas
Anciskes	Anciskes	Panevezys	Kaunas
Anikshet	Anyksciai	Ukmerge	Kaunas
Anishok, Anushishok	Onuskis	Trakai	Vilnius

OLD NAME	CURRENT NAME	UEZD	GUBERNIYA
Anishuk Drom Mizrach	Oniskis	Zarasai	Kaunas
Anishuk Tzfaon Mizrach	Onuskis	Trakai	Vilnius
Antalept, Antilept, Antolepty	Antaliepte	Zarasai	Kaunas
Antokol	Antakalnis	Vilnius	Vilnius
Anturke	Inturke	Vilnius	Vilnius
Anushiskok	Oniskis	Zarasai	Kaunas
Aran	Varena	Trakai	Vilnius
Azarni, Azhran	Zarasai	Zarasai	Kaunas
B			
Bagaslaviskis	Bagaslaviskis	Vilnius	Vilnius
Balbirishki, Balbirishok	Balbieriskis	Marijampole	Suwalki
Balkunai	Varnenai	Vilnius	Vilnius
Baltromants	Butrimonys	Trakai	Vilnius
Barshtitsy	Barstyciai	Telsiai	Kaunas
Batak, Batuk	Batakai	Raseiniai	Kaunas
Bazilyan, Brazilionis	Baziolnai	Siauliai	Kaunas
Beisagala	Baisogola	Siauliai	Kaunas
Bershitz	Barstyciai	Telsiai	Kaunas
Betigola	Betygala	Kaunas	Kaunas
Bezdany	Bezdonys	Vilnius	Vilnius
Birzhi, Birze, Birche	Birzai	Panevezys	Kaunas
Bobt, Bobty, Bobet	Babtai	Kaunas	Kaunas
Bogoslavishik	Bogaslavas	Vilnius	Vilnius
Bolniki	Balninkai	Ukmerge	Kaunas
Botka	Batakai	Raseiniai	Kaunas
Botoken	Batakai	Vilnius	Vilnius
Botrimanetz	Butrimonys	Trakai	Vilnius
Butrimants, Butrimonicai	Butrimonys	Trakai	Vilnius
C			
Chabashkis, Chobishok	Ciobiskis	Vilna	Vilnius

OLD NAME	CURRENT NAME	UEZD	GUBERNIYA
Chekishki, Cheishok, Cesiskis	Cekiske	Kaunas	Kaunas
Chveidan, Chveidany	Kvedarna	Raseiniai	Kaunas
Citavjan	Tytuveniai	Raseiniai	Kaunas
D			
Dabeik	Dabekiai	Ukmerge	Kaunas
Dantova	Dotnuva	Kaunas	Kaunas
Darbean, Darbyany	Darbenai	Telsiai	Kaunas
Darshinishok	Darsuniskis	Trakai	Vilnius
Datnove	Dotnuva	Kaunas	Kaunas
Daug, Daugi	Daugai	Trakai	Vilnius
Dauglakis	Dauglakis	Raseiniai	Kaunas
Debeykyay	Debeikiai	Ukmerge	Kaunas
Dobeiki	Debeikiai	Ukmerge	Kaunas
Doig	Daugai	Trakai	Vilnius
Dorbenai, Dorbiany, Dorbjan	Darbenai	Telsiai	Kaunas
Doseat	Dusetos	Zarasai	Kaunas
Drobian, Drobiany	Darbenai	Telsiai	Kaunas
Drozgenik, Druckenik, Druskenik	Druskinikai	Trakai	Vilnius
Duksht, Dukstos	Dukstas	Zarasai	Kaunas
Dusiaty, Dusetai, Dusiat, Dustoi	Dusetos	Zarasai	Kaunas
Duskieniki	Druskinikai	Trakai	Vilnius
E			
Ehishishuk	Eisiskis	Lida	Vilnius
Eirogala	Ariogala	Kaunas	Kaunas
Eishishki, Eishiskok, Ejszyszki	Eisiskis	Lida	Vilnius
Erzhvilki, Erzhvilk, Erzvilek	Erzvilkas	Raseiniai	Kaunas
Ezeranai, Ezheren, Ezreni	Zarasai	Zarasai	Kaunas
G			
Ganushishki	Onuskis	Trakai	Vilnius

106

OLD NAME	CURRENT NAME	UEZD	GUBERNIYA
Garsden, Gashtin	Gargzdai	Telsiai	Kaunas
Gaure, Gavre, Gauvery	Gaure	Raseiniai	Kaunas
Gedrovitch	Giedraiciai	Vilnius	Vilnius
Gelvan, Gelvonys	Gelvonai	Vilnius	Vilnius
Geleziai	Geguzine	Panevezys	Kaunas
Geozgenburg	Jurbarkas	Raseiniai	Kaunas
Giedroiciai	Giedraiciai	Vilnius	Vilnius
Girtakol, Girtagola, Girtigula	Girkalnis	Raseiniai	Kaunas
Glevan, Glevonis, Glevoniai	Gelvonai	Vilnius	Vilnius
Gorgzhdy, Gorzd, Gorzad	Gargzdai	Telsiai	Kaunas
Gorliava, Gudlowa	Garliava	Marijampole	Suwalki
Grinkishki, Grinkishok	Grinskiskis	Kaunas	Kaunas
Grudzhun, Gruzd, Gruzdzi	Grudziai	Siauliai	Kaunas
Gudel, Gudlova	Gudeliai	Marijampole	Suwalki
Gudzhun, Gudson	Gudziunai	Kaunas	Kaunas
H			
Hidotzihok, Hoduciszki	Adutiskis	Vilnius	Vilnius
I			
Iloki, Ilakas	Ylakiai	Telsiai	Kaunas
Intorik	Inturke	Vilnius	Vilnius
Ionishkis	Joniskelis	Panevezys	Kaunas
Irgola	Ariogala	Kaunas	Kaunas
J			
Janischki	Joniskis	Siauliai	Kaunas
Janowo	Jonava	Kaunas	Kaunas
Jasvainiai	Josvainiai	Kaunas	Kaunas
Jaszuny	Jasiunai	Vilnius	Vilnius
Jeziorosy	Ezerenai	Zarasai	Kaunas
Jeziorosy	Zarasai	Zarasai	Kaunas
Jeznas	Jieznas	Trakai	Vilnius

OLD NAME	CURRENT NAME	UEZD	GUBERNIYA
K			
Kadainai	Kedainiai	Kaunas	Kaunas
Kaltinan, Kaltinyan, Koltintnai	Kaltenenai	Raseiniai	Kaunas
Kalvariya, Kalwaria	Kalvarija	Kalvarija	Suwalki
Kalveriye Zhamut	Zemaiciu Kalvarija	Telsiai	Kaunas
Kamje	Kamajai	Zarasai	Kaunas
Kapuskas	Marijampole	Marijampole	Suwalki
Karaimu Naumiestis	Naujamiestis	Panevezys	Kaunas
Karnove	Kernava	Kudirkos Naumiestis	Vilnius
Kavarsk	Kavarskas	Ukmerge	Kaunas
Kazlove Rude	Kazlu Ruda	Kudirkos Naumiestis	Suwalki
Keidan, Keidany	Kedainiai	Kaunas	Kaunas
Kelm, Kelmy	Kelme	Raseiniai	Kaunas
Keltinan	Kaltenenai	Raseiniai	Kaunas
Khveidan	Kvedarna	Raseiniai	Kaunas
Kibart, Kibartz	Kybartai	Vilkaviskis	Suwalki
Kiernowo	Kernava	Kudirkos Naumiestis	Vilnius
Klikol, Kliki, Klykuoliai	Klykoliai	Siauliai	Kaunas
Kodarmah	Kvedarna	Raseiniai	Kaunas
Kok, Kol	Kuliai	Telsiai	Kaunas
Koltininai	Kaltenenai	Raseiniai	Kaunas
Komai, Kemai	Kamajai	Zarasai	Kaunas
Konev	Konev	Lida	Vilnius
Korshan, Korsjan	Kursenai	Siauliai	Kaunas
Kovarsk, Koverskas	Kavarskas	Ukmerge	Kaunas
Kovne, Kowno	Kaunas	Kaunas	Kaunas
Kraki	Krakes	Kaunas	Kaunas
Krakinovo, Krekinovo	Krekenava	Panevezys	Kaunas
Kretingen	Kretinga	Telsiai	Kaunas
Krok, Kroki	Krakiai	Kaunas	Kaunas

OLD NAME	CURRENT NAME	UEZD	GUBERNIYA
Krosna	Krasna	Kalvarija	Suwalki
Krottingen	Kretinga	Telsiai	Kaunas
Krozhi, Kruce, Krush	Kraziai	Raseiniai	Kaunas
Kruk, Kruky, Krukyay	Kriukai	Siauliai	Kaunas
Kruki	Kriukai	Kaunas	Kaunas
Kuidany	Kedainiai	Kaunas	Kaun as
Kul, Kuli	Kuliai	Telsiai	Kaunas
Kupishki, Kupishok	Kupiskis	Ukmerge	Kaunas
Kurshan, Kurshany	Kursenai	Siauliai	Kaunas
Kvati, Kvietiski, Kvetishok	Kvetkai	Zarasai	Kaunas
L			
Labardzai	Labardzai	Raseiniai	Kaunas
Laibiskiai, Leibishok	Laibiskis	Vilnius	Vilnius
Laizevo, Latzuva	Laizuva	Siauliai	Kaunas
Lal, Liolyay	Lioliai	Raseiniai	Kaunas
Latskove, Latzkeva	Leckava	Siauliai	Kaunas
Lavkovo, Laukuba	Laukuva	Telsiai	Kaunas
Leilpolingis	Leipalingis	Sejny	Suwalki
Leipon, Leipuny	Leipalingis	Sejny	Suwalki
Letzkovo, Letzkuva	Leckava	Siauliai	Kaunas
Lidovian	Lyduveniai	Raseiniai	Kaunas
Lidvinova	Liudvinavas	Kalvarija	Suwalki
Ligmian, Lingmyan, Linkmenai	Linkmenys	Svencionys	Vilnius
Ligumy	Ligumai	Siauliai	Kaunas
Linkeve, Linkowo	Linkuva	Panevezys	Kaunas
Lizhva	Laizuva	Siauliai	Kaunas
Loykuva	Laukuva	Telsiai	Kaunas
Lukniki	Luoke	Siauliai	Kaunas
Lukshi, Lokshud	Luksiai	Kudirkos Naumiestis	Suwalki

OLD NAME	CURRENT NAME	UEZD	GUBERNIYA
M			
Maishigola, Mashogola	Maisagola	Vilnius	Vilnius
Malat, Meliat, Moliat, Malyat	Moletai	Vilnius	Vilnius
Mariapol, Marijampolis	Marijampole	Marijampole	Suwalki
Masiadi, Misiad	Mosedis	Telsiai	Kaunas
Mazeikai, Mazheik, Mosejki	Mazeikiai	Sauliai	Kaunas
Meretz, Merts	Merkine	Trakai	Vilnius
Meshkotz, Meshkutzi	Meshkutziai	Siauliai	Kaunas
Mikhaliskis	Mikailiskis	Vilnius	Vilnius
Mosnik	Musninkai	Vilnius	Vilnius
Muravevo, Muzawiewo	Mazeikiai	Sauliai	Kaunas
N			
Naishtot-Saki	Kudirkos Naumiestis	Kudirkos Naumiestis	Vilnius
Naistot-Ponevez	Naujamiestis	Panevezys	Kaunas
Namyun	Nemaniuai	Trakai	Vilnius
Nauja Vilnia	Naujoji Vilnia	Vilnius	Vilnius
Naujadvaris	Novy Dvor	Lida	Vilnius
Nayshtot Shaky	Kudirkos Naumiestis	Kudirkos Naumiestis	Vilnius
Nei Radvilishok	Radviliskis	Panevezys	Kaunas
Nei Vilejka	Naujoji Vilnia	Vilnius	Vilnius
Nei Zhagar, Novye Zahagoy	Novozagare	Siauliai	Kaunas
Neishtat	Kudirkos Naumiestis	Kudirkos Naumiestis	Vilnius
Nemenchin, Nemevzin	Nemencine	Vilnius	Vilnius
Nemoksht, Nemokeshty	Nemaksciai	Raseiniai	Kaunas
Noiye Mesto	Naujamiestis	Panevezys	Kaunas
Novo Vileisk, Nowo Wilejka	Naujoji Vilnia	Vilnius	Vilnius
Novo-Aleksxandrovsk	Zarasai	Zarasai	Kaunas
Nowe Swienciany	Svencioneliai	Svencionys	Vilnius

OLD NAME	CURRENT NAME	UEZD	GUBERNIYA
O			
Obel	Obeliai	Zarasai	Kaunas
Oishpul	Uzpaliai	Ukmerge	Kaunas
Okmian, Okmiyani	Akmene	Siauliai	Kaunas
Oknista	Aknista	Zarasai	Kaunas
Olita	Alytus	Trakai and Kalvaria	Vilnius and Suwalki
Olkenik, Olkeniki	Valkininkai	Trakai	Vilnius
Olsiady	Alsedziai	Telsiai	Kaunas
Onikshty	Anyksciai	Ukmerge	Kaunas
Onuskes	Onuskis	Zarasai	Kaunas
Oran	Varena	Trakai	Vilnius
Otian	Utena	Ukmerge	Kaunas
P			
Paberzhe, Padbradje	Paberze	Vilnius	Vilnius
Pajurys, Payure	Pajuris	Raseiniai	Kaunas
Pakrojas, Pakob	Pakruojis	Panevezys	Kaunas
Palangen	Palanga	Telsiai	Kaunas
Pandelys	Pandelis	Zarasai	Kaunas
Paniemun	Poniemon	Marijampole	Suwalki
Papile	Papilis	Zarasai	Kaunas
Patsinel	Pociuneliai	Kaunas	Kaunas
Payevonis	Pajavoniai	Volkovishki	Suwalki
Pazhvel, Podzhekva	Zelva	Ukmerge	Kaunas
Pineve, Piniyave	Pilviskiai	Marijampole	Suwalki
Plungian, Plungiany	Plunge	Telsiai	Kaunas
Podberezhe	Paberze	Vilnius	Vilnius
Pokroi	Pakruojis	Panevezys	Kaunas
Polaga, Polange, Polangen	Palanga	Telsiai	Kaunas
Pompiani	Pumpenai	Panevezys	Kaunas
Pon, Poon	Punia	Trakai	Vilnius
Ponevezh	Panevezys	Panevezys	Kaunas
Ponideli	Pandelis	Zarasai	Kaunas

OLD NAME	CURRENT NAME	UEZD	GUBERNIYA
Ponovezio Velzis	Panevezys	Panevezys	Kaunas
Popielany, Popilian	Papile	Siauliai	Kaunas
Popil	Papilis	Zarasai	Kaunas
Poshvitin	Pasvitynis	Siauliai	Kaunas
Posvol	Pasvalys	Panevezys	Kaunas
Potzunel	Pociuneliai	Kaunas	Kaunas
Poyuri	Pajuris	Raseiniai	Kaunas
Pozelvy	Pazelviai	Ukmerge	Kaunas
Pren, Preny, Priyenay	Prienai	Marijampole	Suwalki
Pumpyan	Pumpenai	Panevezys	Kaunas
Pundil, Punidel	Pandelis	Zarasai	Kaunas
Pusholat	Pusalotus	Panevezys	Kaunas
R			
Radvilishki, Radvilishok	Radviliskis	Siauliai	Kaunas
Ragola	Ariogala	Kaunas	Kaunas
Rakishki, Rakishok	Rokiskis	Zarasai	Kaunas
Rasin, Rasseyn	Raseinai	Raseinai	Kaunas
Ratnicza	Ratnycia	Trakai	Kaunas
Remigola	Ramygala	Panevezys	Kaunas
Rimshany	Rimse	Zarasai	Kaunas
Ritove, Rietuva	Rietevas	Raseiniai	Kaunas
Rodamin	Rudamina	Kalvarija	Suwalki
Rodoneh	Raduone	Lida	Vilnius
Rogove, Rogovo, Roguva	Raguva	Ukmerge	Kaunas
Romshishok	Rumsiskes	Kaunas	Kaunas
Rossieny	Raseinai	Raseinai	Kaunas
Rukainiai, Rukojne	Rukoiniai	Vilnius	Vilnius
Rumshishki, Rumsiske	Rumsiskes	Kaunas	Kaunas
S			
Sakai, Saki, Szaki	Sakiai	Kudirkos Naumiestis	Suwalki
Salant, Salanty	Salantai	Telsiai	Kaunas

OLD NAME	CURRENT NAME	UEZD	GUBERNIYA
Salat, Salatas, Salaty	Salociai	Panevezys	Kaunas
Salatznik, Soletchnik	Salcininkeliai	Vilnius	Vilnius
Sapiezyszki, Sapizishok. Spizishok	Zapyskis	Marijampole	Suwalki
Saray, Sarhei, Serhei	Serijai	Sjeini	Suwalki
Sardanik, Sardnok	Seredzius	Kaunas	Kaunas
Sarhei	Sierijai	Siauliai	Kaunas
Sartyniki	Sartininkai	Raseiniai	Kaunas
Sedy, Siad	Seda	Telsiai	Kaunas
Seiny	Seinai	Sejni	Suwalki
Semeliskiai, Semilishuk	Semeliskis	Trakai	Vilnius
Sereje, Sereheya	Serijai	Sjeini	Suwalki
Sesoliai	Sesuoliai	Vilnius	Vilnius
Shadove	Seduva	Panevezys	Kaunas
Shashol	Sesuoliai	Vilnius	Vilnius
Shat, Shaty	Seta	Ukmerge	Kaunas
Shavkeany	Saukenai	Siauliai	Kaunas
Shavlan, Shavlany, Shvelan	Siaulenai	Siauliai	Kaunas
Shavli. Shavel	Siauliai	Siauliai	Kaunas
Shidlovo	Siluva	Raseiniai	Kaunas
Shirvent, Shervinty, Sirvintai	Sirvintos	Vilnius	Vilnius
Shkod, Shkud, Shkudy	Skuodas	Telsiai	Kaunas
Shodina	Siaudine	Kudirkos Naumiestis	Suwalki
Shokian	Saukenai	Kudirkos Naumiestis	Suwalki
Shoshli	Zasliai	Trakai	Vilnius
Shot	Seta	Ukmerge	Kaunas
Shukian	Saukenai	Kudirkos Naumiestis	Suwalki
Shumsk, Sumskas	Sumskai	Kudirkos Naumiestis	Vilnius
Shveksni	Sveksna	Raseiniai	Kaunas
Sialenai	Siaulenai	Siauliai	Kaunas
Silale	Silale	Raseiniai	Kaunas
Siminiai, Simna, Simonas	Simnas	Kalvarija	Suwalki

OLD NAME	CURRENT NAME	UEZD	GUBERNIYA
Sipishok	Snipiskis	Vilnius	Vilnius
Skem, Skemiany, Skimian	Skiemonys	Ukmerge	Kaunas
Skirsnemune	Skirsnemunes	Telsiai	Kaunas
Skomian	Skiemonys	Ukmerge	Kaunas
Skoudvile, Shkudvil	Skaudvile	Raseiniai	Kaunas
Sloboda	Slobodka	Zarasai	Kaunas
Slobodke	Viliampol	Kaunas	Kaunas
Slutznik	Salcininkeliai	Vilnius	Vilnius
Sod	Seda	Telsiai	Kaunas
Sokian	Saukenai	Kudirkos Naumiestis	Suwalki
Soloki, Salok., Sluk	Salakas	Zarasai	Kaunas
Somloshuk	Semeliskis	Trakai	Vilnius
Spatses	Subacius	Ukmerge	Kaunas
Sredniki. Strednius	Seredzius	Kaunas	Kaunas
Statliskes	Stoklishok	Trakai	Vilnius
Stojaciska	Svencionys	Svencionys	Vilnius
Stoklishok	Stakliskes	Trakai	Vilnius
Subotsh	Subacius	Ukmerge	Kaunas
Sudarg, Sudargai	Sudargas	Kudirkos Naumiestis	Suwalki
Suidine	Sakiai	Kudirkos Naumiestis	Suwalki
Sumelish	Semeliskis	Trakai	Vilnius
Surilishok	Surviliskis	Kaunas	Kaunas
Suveinishki, Sovainishuk	Suvainiskis	Zarasai	Kaunas
Suveinishki, Suyeinishok	Surviliskis	Kaunas	Kaunas
Svenchan, Svintson, Shvintzion	Svencionys	Svencionys	Vilnius
Svidostch, Svaidushet	Svedasiai	Ukmerge	Kaunas
Swakiany	Saukenai	Kudirkos Naumiestis	Suwalki
Sweiciany	Svencionys	Svencionys	Vilnius
T			
Taujenu, Tauyenay, Tavian	Taujenai	Ukmerge	Kaunas
Taurogen	Taurage	Raseiniai	Kaunas

OLD NAME	CURRENT NAME	UEZD	GUBERNIYA
Taurogen. Taurogi	Tauragnai	Zarasai	Kaunas
Tavrig, Tavrik	Taurage	Raseiniai	Kaunas
Tavroginy, Tavrog, Targin	Tauragnai	Zarasai	Kaunas
Tchiobiski	Ciobiskis	Vilnius	Vilnius
Telshi, Telsh, Telsze, Telz	Telsiai	Telsiai	Kaunas
Tirkshli, Tirkslah	Tirksliai	Telsiai	Kaunas
Tovrik	Taurage	Raseiniai	Kaunas
Tovyany, Towiany	Taujenai	Ukmerge	Kaunas
Traken	Trakai	Trakai	Vilnius
Trashkon, Traszkuny,	Troskunai	Ukmerge	Kaunas
Traupe, Treip	Traupis	Ukmerge	Kaunas
Trishki, Trishig. Trishik	Tryskiai	Siauliai	Kaunas
Trok, Troki	Trakai	Trakai	Vilnius
Tsitevyan	Tytuveniai	Raseiniai	Kaunas
Turgeli	Turgeliai	Vilnius	Vilnius
Tutavenai	Tytuveniai	Raseiniai	Kaunas
Tver	Tverai	Telsiai	Kaunas
Tvian	Taujenai	Ukmerge	Kaunas
Tzeikishok	Cekiske	Kaunas	Kaunas
U			
Udainiai	Utena	Ukmerge	Kaunas
Upiny, Upenas	Upyna	Raseiniai	Kaunas
Upita	Upyte	Panevezys	Kaunas
Urdomin	Rudamina	Kalvarija	Suwalki
Ushpol, Uzpalis, Uzhventy	Uzpaliai	Ukmerge	Kaunas
Utziany, Utciana, Utian	Utena	Ukmerge	Kaunas
Uzhventy, Uzvent	Uzventis	Siauliai	Kaunas
V			
Vadislavov	Kudirkos Naumiestis	Kudirkos Naumiestis	Vilnius
Vaigovo	Vaiguva	Siauliai	Kaunas
Valeishishok	Valeisiskis	Lida	Vilnius

115

OLD NAME	CURRENT NAME	UEZD	GUBERNIYA
Valkiniki	Olkieniki	Trakai	Vilnius
Varzhian, Verzian	Veivirzeniai	Siauliai	Kaunas
Vashki	Vaskiai	Panevezys	Kaunas
Vegery	Vegeriai	Siauliai	Kaunas
Veiver	Veiveriai	Marijampole	Suwalki
Veivirzhany	Veivirzeniai	Siauliai	Kaunas
Vendziagole	Vanziogala	Kaunas	Kaunas
Verbal, Verblun, Verzhbelov	Virbalis	Vilvaviskis	Suwalki
Vevia, Vevis, Veiver	Veiveriai	Trakai	Vilnius
Vidukli	Vidukle	Raseiniai	Kaunas
Vidzi	Vidziai	Zarasai	Kaunas
Vidziski, Vidishok	Vidiskiai	Vilnius	Vilnius
Viekshny	Vieksniai	Siauliai	Kaunas
Vilamposkaya Sloboda	Viliampol	Kaunas	Kaunas
Vileika	Naujoji Vilnia	Vilnius	Vilnius
Vilkomir, Vilkomerge	Ukmerge	Ukmerge	Kaunas
Vilky	Vilkija	Kaunas	Kaunas
Vilna, Wilno	Vilnius	Vilnius	Vilnius
Virblan	Virbalis	Vilkaviskis	Suwalki
Vishtinets, Vishtinitz	Vistytis	Vilkaviskis	Suwalki
Vivri	Veiveriai	Trakai	Vilnius
Vizhuny	Vyzuonis	Ukmerge	Kaunas
Vobolniki	Vabalninkas	Panevezys	Kaunas
Voinuty	Vainutas	Raseiniai	Kaunas
Voranava	Voranovo	Lida	Vilnius
Vorne, Vorni	Varniai	Telsiai	Kaunas
Vorniany	Varnenai	Vilnius	Vilnius
W			
Wiejsieje	Veisiejai	Sejny	Suwalki
Wierzbelow	Virbalis	Vilvaviskis	Suwalki
Wilkomir, Wilkomerge	Ukmerge	Ukmerge	Kaunas
Wirballen	Virbalis	Vilvaviskis	Suwalki
Wisztyniec, Wishtinits	Vistytis	Vilkaviskis	Suwalki
Wozhy	Varnenai	Vilnius	Vilnius

OLD NAME	CURRENT NAME	UEZD	GUBERNIYA
Y			
Yakubanste	Jokubonys	Vilnius	Vilnius
Yalkai, Yelok, Ylok	Ylakiai	Telsiai	Kaunas
Yaneve	Jonava	Kaunas	Kaunas
Yanishke, Yanishok, ,Yenishki	Joniskis	Panevezys	Kaunas
Yanishkel, Yanishok	Joniskelis	Siauliai	Kaunas
Yashny	Jasiunai	Vilnius	Vilnius
Yasvoini, Yasvainiai, Yasvene	Josvainiai	Kaunas	Kaunas
Yezna	Jieznas	Trakai	Vilnius
Yoganishkeli, Yonishkel	Joniskis	Panevezys	Kaunas
Yoganishkeli, Yonishkel	Joniskelis	Siauliai	Kaunas
Yorburg, Yorvorig, Yurberik	Jurbarkas	Raseiniai	Kaunas
Yosven, Yosvian	Josvainiai	Kaunas	Kaunas
Yurbarkas	Jurbarkas	Raseiniai	Kaunas
Z			
Zager Chadash	Novozagare	Siauliai	Kaunas
Zapishuk	Zapyskis	Marijampole	Suwalki
Zeim, Zeimys	Zeimiai	Kaunas	Kaunas
Zelva	Pazelviai	Ukmerge	Kaunas
Zemaiciu Kalvarija	Kalveriye Zhamut	Kalvarija	Suwalki
Zemaiciu Naumiestis	Zemaiciu Naumiestis	Raseiniai	Kaunas
Zemel, Zheimili	Zeimelis	Panevezys	Kaunas
Zhagar	Zagare	Siauliai	Kaunas
Zharan, Zhorany	Zarenai	Telsiai	Kaunas
Zheimeliany	Zemalenai	Telsiai	Kaunas
Zhidik, Zidik, Zhidiki	Zidkiai	Telsiai	Kaunas
Zosle, Zhushli	Zasliai	Trakai	Vilnius

APPENDIX B

FURTHER READING

BOOKS

Genealogy

Getting Started in Jewish Genealogy by Gary Mokotoff and Warren Blatt Avotaynu, 2000.

Avotaynu Guide to Jewish Genealogy ed. Sallyann Amdur Sack and Gary Mokotoff, 2004

Discovering Your Jewish Ancestors by Barbara Krasner-Khait, North Salt Lake, UT: Heritage Quest, 2001.

Archival resources

Jewish Vital Records, Revision Lists and other Jewish Holdings in the Lithuanian Archives by Harold Rhode and Sallyann Amdur Sack) Avotaynu, 1996.

Various articles published in Avotaynu, some of which are:

- Shadevich, Yakov, "*New Archival Finds from Lithuania*", volume XI, number 2, Summer 1995
- Rhode, Harold, "*Jewish Revision Lists in Lithuanian Archives*", volume XIII, number 3, Fall 1997
- Margol, Howard and Rhode, Harold, "*Kaunas Archives*", volume XIII, number 3, Fall 1997
- Margol, Howard, "*Revelations and New Discoveries in the Vilnius Civil Registry Office,*" volume XIV, number 1, Spring 1998.

- Greenblatt, Ada, *"Lithuanian Central Civil Register Archives Revisited,"* volume XIV, number 1, Spring 1998

Jewish communities and shtetlach in Lithuania

A comprehensive on-line bibliography on the subject of the Jews of Lithuania compiled by Professor Dov Levin can be found at www.isragen.org.il/BIB/lithuania.htm

Lite (Lithuania) (in Yiddish)
- vol 1, Ed. M. Sudarsky, U. Katzenelenbogen, J. Kissin, New York, Jewish-Lithuanian Cultural Society, 1951
- vol, 2 Ed. C.Leikowicz, Tel Aviv, 1965

Yahadut Lita (Lithuanian Jewry) (in Hebrew)
- vol. 1, *Jews of Lithuania to 1918*, eds: N. Goren, L. Garfinkel et al., Tel Aviv, 1959;
- vol. 2, *1918-1941*, eds: R. Hasman, D. Lipec et. al., 1972;
- vol. 3, *People and Places*, eds: R. Hasman, D. Lipec et al., The Association of Lithuanian Jews in Israel: Tel Aviv, 1967;
- vol. 4, *The Holocaust, 1941-1945,* ed: L. Garfunkel, The Association of Lithuanian Jews in Israel, Tel Aviv, 1984

Lithuanian Jewish Communities (Translation of Volume 3 of *Yahadut Lita*) Ed: Nancy and Stuart Schoenberg, New York, 1991

Yiddishe Shtet, Shtetlakh un dorfishe Yishuvim in Lite: biz 1918: historish-biografishe skitses (Jewish cities, towns, and villages in Lithuania), Berl Kagan, New York, 1991 (in Yiddish)

Pinkas Ha-kehillot: Lite , Dov Levin, Yad Vashem (in Hebrew), 1996.

Preserving our Jewish Heritage, Josef Rosin. A History of 31 Jewish communities in Lithuania. (Alytus, Birzai, Jurbarkas, Kaisiadorys, Kapciamiestis, Klaipeda, Kudirkos Naumiestis, Kybartai, Lazdijai, Lygumai, Marijampole, Merkine, Panevezys, Pilviskiai, Prienai, Sakiai, Salantai, Seirijai, Seta, Stakliskes, Sudargas, Taurage, Tauragnai,

Telsiai, Utena, Varena, Veisiejai, Vilkaviskis, Virbalis, Zeimelis, Zemaiciu Naumiestis), 2005

Where Once We Walked: A Guide to the Jewish Communities Destroyed in the Holocaust., Gary Mokotoff and Sallyann Amdur Sack, with Alexander Sharon. Revised Edition. Avotaynu, 2002.

The University of Cape Town's Jewish library has a web-site with searchable databases at www.lib.uct.ac.za/jewish.   One web-page has a bibliography of South African articles written on Litvak *shtetlach*: www.lib.uct.ac.za/jewish/biblio.php3?srcid=1

Vilna (Vilnius)

Vilna, Israel Cohen, Jewish Publication Society of America: Philadelphia and Jerusalem. Originally published 1943 Facsimile edit. 1992.

History

History of the Jews in Russia and Poland, Simon Dubnow, 1918. Republished in one volume by Avotaynu.

The Jews of Lithuania: A History of a Remarkable Community 1316-1945, Masha Greenbaum, 1995.

The Litvaks, A Short History of the Jews of Lithuania, Dov Levin, Yad Vashem, (2nd Ed., English), 2002

Baltic Jews under the Soviets, Dov Levin, Centre for Research & Documentation of Eastern European Jewry, Hebrew University of Jerusalem, 1994

Profiles of A Lost World, Hirsz Abramowicz, 1999

*From a Ruined Garden (*77 selections from Yizkor Books) Ed. Jack Kugelmassand Jonathan Boyarin.

The Holocaust

Holocaust in Lithuania 1941-1945 A Book of Remembrance. Rose Lerer Cohen and Saul Issroff, Gefen: Jerusalem and New York, 2002

The Annihilation of Lithuania Jewry , Rabbi Ephraim Oshry, Judaica Press, Inc.: Brooklyn, NY, 1995 (47 towns listed)

Ghetto in Flames : The Struggle and Destruction of the Jews in Vilna in the Holocaust, Yitzchak Arad   Yad Vashem and ADL Bnai Brith: Jerusalem, 980

The Last Days of the Jerusalem of Lithuania, Herman Kruk, 2002

Surviving the Holocaust: The Kovno Ghetto Diary,   ed: Avram Tory, Harvard University Press, 1990; Pimlico Press, 1991

Kaddish for Kovno: Life and Death in a Lithuanian ghetto 1941-1945, William W. Mishell, Chicago Review Press, 1988

The Yizkor book for Ritavas ed: Alter Levite. (First edition, published in Israel in 1977, was largely in Hebrew and Yiddish. Revised edition, ed. by Dr Dina Porat and Ronib Stauber, translated into English and supplemented by additional articles, published by The Kaplan-Kushlick Foundation, 2000).

How to Document Victims and Locate Survivors of the Holocaust, Gary Mokotoff, Avotaynu 1995. (A large portion is available on-line at www.avotaynu.com/holocaust).

General

Russian-Jewish Given Names: Their Origins and Variants, Boris Feldblyum

AVOTAYNU ARTICLES

Types of archival records
Explains 1795 Revision List VIII/3/66 (1992)
Explains Lithuanian revision lists XII/4/83 (1996)
Researching 18th-Century Census and Tax Lists from the Grand
Duchy of Lithuania   XVII/3/7 (2001)
Collection of Box Taxes in 19th-Century Lithuania XVII/3/43
(2001)

Archival resources
Vital records of Lithuanian Jewry found   VI/2/03 (1990)
Jewish Vital Statistic Records in Lithuanian Archives VI/4/04 (1990)
More about the Lithuanian archives IX/1/65 (1993)
Relates experience with Lithuanian archives IX/1/65 (1993)
New archival finds from Lithuania XI/2/10 (1995)
Archival sources in the Lithuanian State Archives XI/3/03 (1995)
Holdings in the Vilnius archives XII/1/19 (1996)
Jewish revision lists in Vilnius archives XII/2/19 (1996)
Jewish Revision Lists in Lithuanian Archives XIII/3/23 (1997)
Kaunas Archives XIII/3/25 (1997)
Revelations and New Discoveries in the Vilnius Civil Registry Office
XIV/1/21 (1998)
Lithuanian Central Civil Register Archives Revisited XIV/1/22
(1998)
Jewish Genealogical Resources at the Kaunas State Archives
XIV/3/29)1998)
Some Lithuanian Discoveries XVI/1/18 (2000)
Missing Lithuanian Vital Records Found! XVI/4/42 (2000)

General

A Synopsis of 18th-Century Lithuanian-Jewish History XVIII/1/23
(2002)
Using Litvak naming patterns to derive names of unknown ancestors
XI/3/22 (1995)
Jewish Given Names in the Grand Duchy of Lithuania   XIII/2/20
(1997)
Cemetery projects in Latvia and Lithuania XIV/3/69 (1998)

INTERNET ARTICLES

The website of the Miriam Weiner Routes to Roots Foundation, Inc. (www.rtrfoundation.org) carries the following articles on the categories of material available in the various Lithuanian archives

Laima Tautvaisaite: *An Overview of Lithuanian Archives, with a focus on the Lithuanian State Historical Archives.*

Galina Baranova: *A Selected Overview of Documents in the Lithuanian State Historical Archives Pertaining to Jewish Institutions/Organizations.* (See also her article at www.jewishgen.org/Litvak/Galina.htm).

Vitalija Gircyte: *Kaunas Regional Archives*

Dalius Zizys: *Lithuania Central State Archives*

An illuminating contemporary report (1872) on the legal position of "the Hebrews in Russia" by the American Charge d'Affaires in St Petersburg at the time, Eugene Schuyler can be found at www.angelfire.com/ms2/belaroots/schuyler.htm

Yale F Edeiken: *An Introduction to the Einsatzgruppen* http://veritas3.holocaust-history.org/intro-einsatz

The Einsatzgruppen - Mobile Killing Units www.mtsu.edu/%7Ebaustin/einsatz.html

TRAVEL REFERENCES

- "In your pocket" travel guides, available for Vilnius, Kaunas, Klaipėda, Nida, Palanga, Trakai, Druskininkai, Ignalina, Visaginas, Zarasai and Riga. Download free on the web. viyp@post.omnitel.net   http://www.inyourpocket.com
- *Baltic States & Kaliningrad, a travel survival kit* by John Noble, Lonely Planet Publications, 1994.
- *The Baltic States*, Hayit Publishing, 1993.

- *Estonia Latvia & Lithuania* by Nicola Williams, Cathryn Kemp, Debra S. Herrmann 3rd Ed), Lonely Planet, 2003.
- Lithuania, The Bradt Travel Guide by Gordon McLachlan. 3rd ed., Bradt, 2002.
- Baltic Capitals: Tallinn, Riga, Vilnius, Kaliningrad: by Neil Taylor, Bradt Travel Guides, 2001
- *Guide To Lithuania* by Raza Avizienis and William Hough. Editor: Inara Astrida Punga, 1995

INDEX

PUBLICATIONS
IN THE 'JEWISH ANCESTORS' SERIES

Jewish Ancestors?

A Beginner's Guide to Jewish Genealogy in Great Britain
ISBN: 0-9537669-3-4
Series Editor: Rosemary Wenzerul

◆An insight into the world of Jewish genealogy◆
◆A must for the beginner to genealogy◆
◆Packed from cover to cover with useful information◆
◆An inspiration to continue research once started◆

Price: £4.50 + 50p p&p (UK) and £6.00/US$10 (OVERSEAS)

Jewish Ancestors?

A Guide to Jewish Genealogy in Germany and Austria
ISBN: 0-9537669-1-8
Written by: Thea Skyte and Randol Schoenberg
Series Editor: Rosemary Wenzerul

◆ An insight into researching your Germany or Austrian family roots◆
◆An informative guide to the archives of available records◆
◆Explains how to obtain the records you thought no longer existed◆

Price: £4.50 + 50p p&p (UK) and £6.00/US$10 (OVERSEAS)
